THE CASTRATION COMPLEX

THE CASTRATION COMPLEX

What is so Natural about Sexuality?

Mou Sultana

Routledge
Taylor & Francis Group

LONDON AND NEW YORK

First published 2018
by Routledge
2 Park Square, Milton Park, Abingdon, Oxon OX14 4RN

and by Routledge
711 Third Avenue, New York, NY 10017

Routledge is an imprint of the Taylor & Francis Group, an informa business

© 2018 Mou Sultana

British Library Cataloguing-in-Publication Data
A catalogue record for this book is available from the British Library

Library of Congress Cataloging-in-Publication Data
A catalog record has been requested for this book

ISBN: 9781782205807 (pbk)

Typeset in Palatino
by The Studio Publishing Services Ltd
www.publishingservicesuk.co.uk
email: studio@publishingservicesuk.co.uk

CONTENTS

ACKNOWLEDGEMENTS

I would like to express my utmost gratitude to my Masters thesis supervisor, Ms Joanne Conway. Without her unconditional support and dedication neither my thesis nor this book would have happened. I am also hugely indebted to my lecturer and my current PhD supervisor, Dr Barry O'Donnell for his wisdom and guidance. My biggest learning has come from my clinical work, for which I am grateful to my clinical supervisor, Dr Cormac Gallagher. Finally, I would like to thank my family and friends for helping me on my journey in their own unique ways.

ABOUT THE AUTHOR

Mou Sultana is a practising psychotherapist and a psychoanalyst registered with the Irish Council of Psychotherapy (ICP), based in Limerick, Ireland. She works in her private clinic, and with Limerick Youth and Adult Probation Services. She also works as a psycho-therapist providing mental support to hospital staff in Limerick. Prior to her career in psychotherapy, she had been working as a successful singer–songwriter, actress, and television presenter in India. Language and its effect on human subjectivity has always been a keen interest of hers, but it was only pursued after she relocated to Ireland. She completed her Bachelors degree in Integrative Counselling and Psychotherapy with distinction. She also achieved a higher diploma in Psychotherapy Studies and a Diploma in Cognitive–Behavioural Therapy. In addition to this, she received distinction in both her Masters in Sociology from the University of Limerick (UL) and in Psychoanalytic Psychotherapy from University College Dublin (UCD). Her UL thesis is titled, "We know what it is wrong with you and we know how to fix it: DSM, CBT and the making of the neoliberal subject". Her UCD thesis is titled "The castration complex: the myths of sexuality". This book is an extension of her latter thesis. Currently, she is working on her doctoral studies at the School of Medicine in

University College Dublin. Her thesis explores perinatal psychiatric disorders and their relation to the psychoanalytic notion of femininity. When not working, studying, or writing, she enjoys travelling with her husband and two children, preferably to a warmer climate with a beach nearby.

Introduction

This book examines the psychoanalytic notion of the castration complex and its relation to human psychosexual development. Castration is both central and necessary for the formation of the human subject in psychoanalysis. This book illustrates how that is the case. It is the subjective responses to the phenomenon of castration that influences the subject's future relation to the Other and the Law, the formation of the subject's structure, and their acquisition of sexual characteristics. For Freud, "pure masculinity and femininity" are "theoretical constructions of uncertain content" (1925j, p. 258). Moreover, this is "biological phraseology" that psychoanalysis uses as a foundation on which to develop further the concepts of masculine and feminine positions via the theories of the drive and object choice (1920g, p. 171).

Similarly, for Lacan, "man" and "woman" are signifiers, which have remained unwritten from the dawn of civilisation; they exist in the realm of the real and can only be approached along the pathway of the symbolic (1972, Lesson VI) "Man" or "Woman". These terms are confusing, but attempting to define what is a man or a woman is even more baffling. The following chapters illustrate that castration brings an end to these confusions so that the subject can take up a position which is highly subjective but in no manner is this phenomenon of becoming a "sexed subject" "natural" or a "given", as contemporary discourse claims.

Freud's starting point was the examination of the relation between infantile sexuality and adult sexuality. From clinical experiences, he began to develop interest in both establishing the concept of infantile sexuality and enquiring into it. The earlier papers of Freud (Chapter One) highlight the connection between infantile sexuality and adult sexual life. In this process, particularly, Freud was struck by the notion of the castration complex and its impact on Little Hans (1909b). During the 1920s, the emphasis in Freud's work shifted from the similarities between infantile sexuality and adult sexuality to the development of human sexuality. By then, the cornerstone of psychoanalysis, the Oedipus complex, had already been well established. However, there was a major problem. The theory of the Oedipus complex did not fit so well with the notion of the little girl's psychosexual development. This is because the castration complex lies at the heart of the Oedipus complex.

The issue of castration became a major hindrance in smoothly outlining and establishing one whole psychosexual developmental theory, or even two separate ones. In the mid 1920s, Freud was, thus, examining the relation between the Oedipus complex and the castration complex. This particular era of Freud's investigation into psychosexuality highlights the close connections between the castration complex and the difference between the sexes, something Freud already begun to notice in his earlier works concerning childhood research into sexual matters. However, this time, Freud's investigation shows that the question of castration is at the heart of human sexuality and the difference between the sexes are inseparable from the question of castration (Grigg, 1999, p. 11). This is captured in Chapter Two by closely examining the Freudian text, "Some psychical consequences of the anatomical distinction" (1925j). Freud's formulation of the psychosexual theories triggered the major debate famously known as the Freud–Jones debate around the question of female sexuality during the 1920s and 1930s, which has not been included in its entirety in this book, although Freud's responses to the debate have been highlighted on several occasions. Freud responded to the theories and issues raised in the debate and revised his own theories of female sexuality in the 1930s. Such responses are captured in "Female sexuality" (1931b), and Lecture XXXIII of *New Introductory Lectures on*

Psycho-analysis: "Femininity" (1933a). Chapters Three and Five closely examine these two texts.

If 1923–1925 was the era in which Freud articulated the *outcome* of the Oedipus complex for the little girl, the revised theories on female sexuality between 1931–1933 can be regarded as the little girl's *entry* into the Oedipus complex (Grigg, 1999, p. 12). Chapter Four is a collection and summary of Freud's response to, and position regarding, the theory of bisexuality from various stages of his career.

Chapter Five engages with some of Lacan's revisions of the Freudian theories of castration complex. Two of Lacan's lectures on the subject of castration and the Oedipus complex from his Seminar IV are closely examined. Lacan, too, examines the theory of castration complex using the little Hans case.

Based on the findings from all of these chapters, Chapter Six explores the fate of the infantile sexual research questions. Using some of Lacan's lectures dated one year before and one year after his Seminar IV, the final chapter tackles the major question: what can we learn from Lacan's theory of castration about the subject's acquisition of sex?

This book illustrates that, for Freud, not only the castration complex is at the heart of the distinction between the sexes, but also the subjective negotiation of this distinction has an impact on the future sexual positions taken up (or not) by the subject. Sexual difference belongs to the realm of the Real in the Lacanian sense because it resists symbolisation (Gerovichi, 2010). Any attempt at symbolising this difference will always fail to capture the complete understanding of sexual difference. However, since we begin from a polymorphously perverse position and in the psyche there is no distinction between the sexes to begin with, I propose the following.

For the construction of subjectivity and for the child's future development, it is essential that these distinctions between the sexes are recognisable to the child at an elementary level. Such an environment provides a solid foundation, as it marks the child with limitations— limitations that both Freud's and Lacan's theories would describe as castration. Since castration is necessary for the construction of the sexed subject, it is essential that efforts are made at the beginning of life to explain sexual differences to the child, even though such differences will always escape symbolisation. It is this structural impossibility that is at the core of the construction of a subject for both

Freud and Lacan. For Freud, the castration complex is the secret of the distinction between the sexes (Grigg, 1999, p.12) while, for Lacan, castration introduces the subject to his very existence as a sexed being. Engaging with some of the core texts of both Freud and Lacan, this book illustrates how these two revolutionary theorists came to such conclusions.

In essence, this book provides an elementary platform for the students of psychoanalysis and psychotherapy, and to anyone who is interested in a psychoanalytic investigation into human sexuality. Often, psychotherapy students struggle to find a particular topic due to Freud's excessive use of footnotes and his revision of theories throughout his career, which are scattered across the twenty-four volumes of the *Standard Edition*. Similarly, Lacan's enigmatic teaching style and his terminologies too often seem a barrier to students. Often, students prefer to read secondary texts as an escape. With this in mind, I have chosen a handful of texts and read them closely with the hope that it will encourage others to read Freud and Lacan's work as primary texts. To those who are familiar with Freud and Lacan, the omission of Freud's theories on death drive, Lacan's formulation of desire, *jouissance*, and sexuation in this book might come as a surprise. The aim was to make theories of Freud and Lacan accessible to a wide variety of readers from all walks of life. Hence, the theories have been presented using more accessible language while, at the same time, the utmost effort has been made to keep their essence intact. Considering that both castration and sexuality are foundational topics in psychoanalysis, this book is to be considered as only an introduction to the relation between these two.

Since one of my biggest objectives was to highlight how a psychoanalytic investigation into sexuality vastly differs from any other discipline, I have purposely kept the use of terms such as gender, identity, and sexual orientation to a minimum. Instead, I have used the term *sexual position* in order to highlight that, within the context of psychoanalysis, the acquisition of sexuality is a phenomenon of the subject *taking* up a position (or not), as opposed to the idea of the subject being *given* his or her sexuality by nature, biology, anatomy, or society. Sexuality in psychoanalysis is a symptom that reveals something of the person's subjectivity and the very construction of sexuality occurs under the influence of the workings of our unconscious, our mental life.

CHAPTER ONE

The castration complex for Freud between 1907 and 1909

Introduction

This chapter will illustrate how, between 1907 and 1909, while the castration complex was at its inception stage, Freud perceived it as a moment where one infantile sexual theory of the universal existence of the penis is replaced with another: girls have been castrated (Evans, 1996, p. 21). At this stage, the castration complex was described by Freud as the discovery of anatomical differences that brings the necessary end to the sexual puzzlement of children and paves the way for their further psychosexual development. This is because only the discovery of the sexual differences allows children to enter the stage of the Oedipus complex where, subsequently, they acquire the psychical masculine and feminine characteristics that Freud found impossible to define. This phase in Freud's formulation is examined by focusing on two Freudian texts from 1907 and 1908, respectively, wherein versions of the castration complex are found in their earliest form.

Castration and childhood sexual researches

Interpretation of Dreams (1900a) and *Three Essays on the Theory of Sexuality* (1905d) are the foundational texts in psychoanalysis. In particular, *Three Essays on the Theory of Sexuality* is considered by most scholars, and readers in general, as a text which redefined human sexuality forever. This text was originally published in 1905, comprising eighty pages. Freud returned to this text throughout his career (even as late as twenty years or more in some instances) in order to edit, add to, and re-edit his theories on sexuality. The current edition of the *Three Essays on the Theory of Sexuality* comprises 122 pages. The theory of the castration complex was not included in the original version of the text. In the Editor's note to "The infantile genital organization" (1923e, p. 140), James Strachey confirmed that the entire Section 5 of the second essay on infantile sexuality, titled "The sexual researches of childhood" (Freud, 1905d, pp. 194–197) and Section 6 of the same, titled "The phases of development of the sexual organization" (Freud 1905d, pp. 197–200) were added to *Three Essays on the Theory of Sexuality* in 1915. According to Strachey's footnote found in *Three Essays on the Theory of Sexuality* (1905d, p. 194), these additions were based on Freud's later findings that are published in two of Freud's texts, titled "The sexual enlightenment of children (An open letter to Dr. M Furst)" (1907c) and "On the sexual theories of children" (1908c). Most of what has been captured by Freud in these two texts is primarily based on Freud's observation of children, with one child in particular, Little Hans, contributing a lot. In another footnote to the *Three Essays on the Theory of Sexuality* (1905d, p. 135), Strachey verifies that during the drafting of these two texts dated 1907 and 1908, respectively, Little Hans' analysis was, indeed, in progress.

While Little Hans' case (1909b) carries the first published *discussion* of the castration complex in Freud's work (Laplanche & Pontalis, 1973, p. 56), the first ever *appearance* of the terms "castration complex" and "the threat of castration" was, in fact, in "On the sexual theories of children" (1908c, p. 217). Although the idea of a threat of castration was fleetingly mentioned for the very first time in a single sentence of Freud's in his *Interpretation of Dreams* (1900a, p. 619), in relation to Zeus, the term was not discussed until 1908 (see 1908c, p. 217, fn.). This indicates that, while Freud's *Three Essays on the Theory of Sexuality* (1905d) is the most essential thesis to understand infantile sexuality, it was the case of Little Hans that allowed Freud to conclude the following.

The sexual researches of children are not only essential to an understanding of human psychosexual development but also, the theories that children develop in these researches have an impact (1) "upon later neuroses", (2) affect the outcome of their sexual researches, and (3) influence the development of the child's intellectual capability (see 1905d, pp. 195–196, fn. 2). As Hans' analysis progressed, Freud documented most of his theories on the subjects of infantile sexuality and children's sexual researches in these two texts (1907c, 1908c). This might explain why Freud often interchanged the order of the two great questions that children are perplexed by at an "unexpectedly early age": the origin of babies and the distinction between the sexes (1907c, p. 134). The following sections are close readings of these two texts that will illustrate how the concept of castration is enmeshed with the childhood riddles of sex.

In "The sexual enlightenment of children (An open letter to Dr. M Furst)" (1907c), Freud responded to three questions: (1) should children be given the facts of sexual life, (2) if so, then at what age should this be communicated to them, and (3) in what manner should this be communicated? While Freud admitted that the second and the third questions certainly require further discussion, he could not to see any valid reason behind "difference of opinion on the first point" (1907c, p. 131). Referring to the *Three Essays on the Theory of Sexuality* (1905d), and especially to his theories on infantile sexuality, infantile polymorphously perverse disposition, and auto-erotism, Freud argued that

> except for his reproductive power, a child has a fully developed capacity for love long before puberty; and it may be asserted that the "mystery-making" merely prevents him from being able to gain an intellectual grasp of activities for which he is psychically prepared and physically adjusted. (1907c, p. 134)

This is the first instance of Freud placing the question of origin as second to the problem of "distinction between the sexes" (see 1907c, p. 135, fn. 2).

According to Freud, the primacy of the male organ, the penis, in childhood is responsible for children's negligence of the anatomical differences between the sexes: "*attributing to everyone, including females, the possession of a penis*, such as the boy knows from his own body" (1908c, p. 215). Freud highlights this problem of "sex distinction" in children and its tormenting effect by illustrating some of the significant moments from Little Hans' case history (1909b). The first example that Freud provided was the illustration of Hans' "liveliest interest" in his "widdler": "When he was only three he asked his mother: 'Mummy, have you got a widdler too?' His mother answered: 'Of course. What did you think?' He also asked his father the same question repeatedly" (1907c, p. 134).

Freud did not comment on the mother's part in the muddling up of the sexual distinction at this stage and he carried on illustrating other examples of Hans' widdler curiosities. Why did Freud not comment on the mother's response? At the end of the paragraph, he made an overall comment that is crucial in understanding what "sex distinction" means for Freud in Little Hans' case. Freud noted that

> Little Hans is not a sensual child or at all pathologically disposed. The fact is simply, I think, that, *not having been intimidated or oppressed with a sense of guilt*, he gives expression quite ingenuously to what he thinks. (1907c, p. 135, my italics)

The very use of the word *guilt* indicates the presence of an act that is mischievous, naughty, or perhaps forbidden. Perhaps it is an enjoyment that has remained uninterrupted. Perhaps the words *guilt*, *intimidated*, and *oppressed* indicate the very existence of an enjoyment in Hans which is in need of regulation. In the case history, it seems that the father within the family failed to establish a *sense of guilt* in Little Hans, while the mother was left in her position to continue to be the source of (*guilt*-y) pleasure for Little Hans. This is a question of differentiating the role of the father from that of the mother's. Such differentiation of roles would allow a twofold-function to occur: (1) interrupt the enjoyment of both the child and the mother, and (2) install "guilt" in the child so that the child can learn to express "what he thinks" more dis-"ingenuously" in future. In other words, Freud is alluding here to the fact that it is the father who draws the line in the sand, but he does not use the term "father". Moreover, Hans' parents must have been perceived by Freud as neither intimidating nor oppressive, as the above quote suggests; rather, Freud described them as "understanding parents" (1907c, p. 134). It can be argued that Freud's future emphasis on the role of the father that would later become the nucleus of the castration complex in fact finds its roots right here in this comment.

In this same 1907 text, Freud further added that "the origin of babies" is the second great problem with which children struggle (1907c, p. 135). Freud changed this view subsequently, in 1908, and wrote that "the first, grand problem of life" is a question the child asks himself, "Where do babies come from?" (1908c, p. 212). In 1909, Freud again reverted and acknowledged that the origin of babies is the first great problem that children encounter (1909b, p. 133). In 1915, Freud added that not only is this the first riddle that a child is faced with, but also this first problem is in line with the drive's origin (1905d, p. 195) because it is the arrival of a new baby that makes the child fearful of losing his place. Subsequently, in 1925, Freud changed his mind again, based on his clinical observations, and published an article initially titled "Anatomical sex-distinction" (1925j, p. 247), which is, essentially, a synthesis of his theories on sexual development from various stages of his career. Interestingly, the central theme of the 1925j text is castration and a detailed reading of this text is provided in the following chapter. Already, it is becoming evident that there is an intimate connection between sex distinction, sexual distinction (i.e., distinction between the sexes), and the theory of castration.

Freud was working on providing a theoretical framework in which to situate his findings on human sexuality. At this early stage of his formulation, Freud was not only struggling to put the two questions in their right order, but he also had a further layer of complexity to contend with: separating boys and girls into two discrete categories of sexual positions. The biggest obstacle to his formulations was the question of the feminine. The lack of a penis in girls was proving to be a difficult concept to integrate into the theories of castration. In 1908, Freud wrote that, due to "unfavourable circumstances, both of an external and internal nature", the observations documented in "On the sexual theories of children" can be applied only to the question of sexual development of boys (1908c, p. 211). Freud did not stop there, but continued on his quest. On a long, winding path of discoveries and postulating theories on female psychosexual development, there are times when he assumed that the psychology of women is parallel to men's and, later on, there were others that proposed a very different and complicated route to sexual development for women. This sentence is a reference to the succinct summary of Freud's development on the theories of female sexuality written by Strachey, found in the Editor's note of "Some sexual consequences of the anatomical distinction between the sexes" (1925j, pp. 243–247). Albeit, Freud found women more enigmatic than men as Jones suggested (Jones, 1955, p. 468, cited in Freud, 1925j, p. 244, fn. 1) and it is truly captured in Freud's comment, "... the sexual life of adult women is a 'dark continent' for psychology" (1926e, p. 212).

Typical sexual theories of children

In this book, as we progress, it will be evident that the question of the feminine sex is one that brings the subject closer to a confrontation with the real in the Lacanian sense. Real is the domain where symbolisation fails, signification does not hold, and, despite every effort at defining the object, something of the definition always escapes. Such is evident in Freud's comment, documented by Jones, "the great question that has never been answered and which I have not been able to answer, despite my thirty years of research into the feminine soul, is 'what does a woman want?'" (Jones, 1955, p. 468). Freud is not alone here. This is probably echoed by most of human civilisation. But, as we shall see, it finds its primitive expression in childhood sexual researches.

This is also echoed by Lacan, who wrote in his Seminar III on the psychoses that "When Dora finds herself wondering, What is a woman?, she is attempting to symbolize the female organ as such" (Lacan, 1993, p. 178). "Becoming a woman and wondering what a woman is are two essentially different things" (Lacan, 1993, p. 178), according to Lacan, but is it only a question posed by the male sex? This question will be further explored in the last chapter of this book, where we closely examine Lacan's position with regard to castration and its relation to the acquisition of sex. For now, it is essential that we highlight the following.

The question of the feminine identity is not just a woman's question but every hysteric's question, irrespective of their anatomical sex and it is not surprising that it is the *very* question that Freud was himself puzzled by throughout his career. The term "hysteric", in this context, is not to be mistaken for a colloquial demeaning term. It is referred to here in the sense of the clinical structure of the subject (for details, see Chapter Seven). At a very structural level of hysteria lies the question "what is a woman?" and the same seems to be Freud's question, too. The hysteric also asks "Am I a man or a woman?" which, it can be argued, is a refined version of the same question of the feminine sex. Moreover, "Who am I?" and "Where do I come from?" "How did I get here?" are the most existential questions of all. These are questions of "being", questions of our very existence and questions of procreation.

Similar to the question of the feminine sex, procreation is also another definition that slips away and escapes symbolisation (see Chapter Seven). "How do I tell them apart?" and "Where do babies come from?" are the two most troubling questions of children in their sexual researches. I argue that, at a fundamental level, the hysteric's questions and the existential questions of the human race in general are, essentially, more sophisticated versions of these infantile questions. What happens to these questions as we grow up? In the process of these questions becoming more sophisticated, do they effect our "being"? If yes, then how do these question influence the very construction of our subjectivity, our individuality, and our sexuality? Most importantly, how do we answer these questions?

For both Freud and Lacan, the neurotic subject is divided. Freud uses the term *Spaltung* to highlight the separations of the psychical apparatus, such as conscious/pre-conscious–unconscious, or divisions between agencies such as id, ego, and superego. Splitting is described as a result of the subject's inner conflicts (Laplanche & Pontalis, 1973, p. 428). Lacan denotes it as $, the barred subject. Lacanian theorist Verhaeghe (2000, p. 136) suggests that these moments of division occur when children are confronted with existential questions which are threefold in nature: (1) sexual differences, especially female sexual identity, (2) the origin of the subject, that is, the role of the father or the question of authority, and (3) the sexual relation between the parents. These three moments that Verhaeghe (2000) outlined as fundamental moments of subject formation correspond with the three typical sexual theories that Freud outlined in the current text in hand, "On the sexual theories of children" (1908c). The following section illustrates the connections between them.

At this early phase of conceptualising the theory of castration, Freud associated the castration complex with the primacy of the penis in both sexes. Although the term "phallic stage", which is central to the theory of the castration complex, made its first appearance only in 1923, one of the earliest versions of the phallic stage is illustrated in this 1908 text. The phallic stage is elaborated in Chapter Two, where the discussion focuses on Freud's formulation of the castration complex between 1923 and 1925. For now, very briefly, the phallic stage in this Freudian context is described as the stage where partial drives become unified "under the primacy of the genital organs" (Laplanche & Pontalis, 1973, p. 309). This is a phase where, irrespective of his or her anatomical sex, the child knows only one genital organ, the penis.

The following is the beginning of the formation of the phallic stage. Freud noted that infantile sexual theories begin from the neglect of the differentiation between the sexes and the child attributing a penis to everyone. He explained that this is because, for the boy, the penis is "the leading erotogenic zone and the chief auto-erotic sexual object" and this is reflected in the boy's "inability to imagine a person like himself who is without this essential constituent" (1908c, p. 215). The fact that children attribute a penis to everyone at early years of their lives is evident in Hans' following comment regarding his sister, Hanna, "But her widdler's still quite small . . . When she grows up it'll get bigger alright" (1909b, p. 11). Freud insisted that his father must tell Hans that women do not possess a penis. Freud's insistence indicates the beginnings of the formulation of his theory of castration.

Freud's later formulation of the phallic stage confirms that he equated children's knowledge of the anatomical differences as the effect of castration (Laplanche & Pontalis, 1973, p. 309). Hence, Freud's insistence that the father enlighten Hans on sexual differences can be considered as Freud insisting that Hans' father take up the position of the castrating father.

In the case of the girl, however, Freud was not so clear in his formulations. He suggested that the clitoris is equivalent to a small penis and, similar to the boy, the clitoris "becomes the seat of excitations" (1908c, p. 217). This comment tallies with his theory of the primacy of the penis . Much of the following is best redeveloped in his 1925 text (see Chapter Two), but Freud's later formulations of a masculinity complex in women and penis envy are found in their earliest forms right here in this current text. Freud suggested that the girl's clitoral enjoyment could be interpreted as her masculine character which, unless repressed in puberty, would persist (1908c, p. 217).

Also, that her initial interest in the boy's genital soon transforms into envy. The girl feels "she would rather be a boy", experiences "deficiency", and believes that she has been treated unfairly (1908c, p. 218). These moments of childhood bafflement correspond with the question of identity. Questions such as "What is the difference between a man and a woman?", "Am I a man?", "What am I?" might essentially lead to puzzlement about the feminine identity, particularly "What is a woman?"

Freud's second typical sexual theory of children was their questions around "Where do babies come from?" Even when they realise that babies come from the mother's body, children wonder about how the baby got *into* the mother's body. Although they suspect the father's involvement in this, especially that the matter must concern the father's penis, the boy's wish to sustain his belief that the mother does possess a penis soon leads him to "reject and forget" this theory (1908c, pp. 218–219). Hence, the ignorance of the existence of the vagina leads children to believe *"the baby must be evacuated like a piece of excrement, like a stool"* (1908c, p. 219).

Little Hans came up with this alternative theory, faced with the riddle of "the origin of babies". Freud wrote that "he therefore inferred that Hanna had been inside his mother's body, and had then come out like a 'lumf'" (1909b, p. 133). These moments correspond with the question of the role of the father and his function. To a child, the mother's position in relation to the baby might be a bit more clear than the father's. The situation might seem to be, "I can see Mummy's tummy get bigger when there is a baby, but what does daddy do to get the baby?" If the father's involvement, his role or function, is not so clear, the child might make up his own myths. This is evident throughout the case of Little Hans, especially as Hans refused to believe the myth that the stork brought Hanna and formulated his own theories on the origin of babies. His alternative theories, such as that he could give birth just as women do and have his own children, correspond to the fact that Hans was puzzled by the question of the father's function and also about his own position in relation to his father. This is evident in the case study where Hans questions his father about men having children and wishes to situate himself in regard to his father, "Hans: 'But why don't *you* have one? Oh yes, you'll have one all right. Just you wait.' "I: 'I shall have to wait some time.'" "Hans: 'But I belong to you.'" (Freud, 1909b, p. 87). This is not only a moment that highlights Hans' lack of knowledge with regard to anatomical distinction between the sexes, but also of the distinction between the sexes' function in relation to the question of birth. Hans does not know how he belongs to his father. What function does his father have in his life? Moreover, this moment also highlights Hans' refusal to give up his theory of women possessing a penis. This refusal to accept that a woman does not have a penis is further explored in the following chapters.

The third typical sexual theory that children formulate is in relation to the accidental sight of the parental coitus. Whether they observe the sexual positions ("positions" here referring to the literal meaning of the term), or the noises, or any other detail of the act, children usually perceive the phenomenon of parental sexual union as a "sadistic view of coition" (1908c, p. 220). Rather than using this new-found information in the riddle of the origin of the babies as a missing piece, children overlook it and interpret sexual intercourse as an act of violence. These moments correspond with the question of the sexual relationship.

Freud posited many reasons for children adopting this theory, such as children assuming that the usual parental quarrel is continuing at night, or children might theorise the occasional spotting on the bed as the result of an "assault" on the mother caused by the father at night, etc. Most importantly, Freud linked the development of this sadistic theory of coitus in children to their "innate components of the sexual instinct" and their "premature sadistic impulse" (1908c, p. 221). He even implied that the obscure memories of parental coitus might lead to the development of the sadistic impulse instead of the sadistic instinct leading to the development of the theory of the sadistic theory of coitus (1908c, p. 221). It is evident that, faced with the riddles of sexuality during the early years of life, children turn towards myth. This is why Freud examined the myths that the children use to make sense of sexual knowledge. In other words, following Lacan, it can be added that the signifiers, man or woman, and the definition of sex, sexuality, and sexual relations belong to the domain of the real, where signification fails. However, myths belong to the symbolic and they provide the child with the necessary anchoring he needs. When children are faced with the riddles of sexuality, it is myths that they turn to in order to symbolise and make sense of the essential and fundamental questions about human existence.

Oedipal myth

These moments of puzzlement, however, are necessary for psychical development. Freud wrote that, even though the "grown-ups" withhold information, children's secret research continues (1908c, p. 214), but along this path, the first occasion of "psychical conflict arises" (1908c, p. 214). That which feels "good" or "right" to the child seems to contradict the grown-ups' view. Such is the instance when Little Hans invited his mother to play with his "widdler" and he was rejected and told that that would be "piggish!". According to Freud, "psychical conflict" turns into "psychical disassociation" and soon, the "good", the acceptable, and the right "become the dominant and conscious views", while the other set which contains the child's research work, the "obtained fresh evidence which are not supposed to count, become the suppressed and 'unconscious' ones. The nucleus complex of a neurosis is in this way brought into being" (1908c, p. 214). This comment from 1908 not only shows that the formations of psychical components are dependent on these early moments of puzzlement, but also this comment marks the earliest formulation of the Oedipus complex. Strachey noted that the term "Nuclear complex" is, indeed, the earliest form of what Freud later named as the "Oedipus complex" in "A special type of choice of object made by men" (1910h, p. 171; 1908c, p. 214, fn. 1). Just two years after he refers to this phenomena as the "nuclear complex", Freud wrote,

> He begins to desire his mother . . . and to hate his father anew as a rival who stands in the way of this wish; he comes, as we say, under the dominance of the Oedipus complex. He does not forgive his mother for having granted the favour of sexual intercourse not to himself but to his father, and he regards it as an act of unfaithfulness. (1910h, p. 171)

The oedipal myth provided Freud with the much needed framework within which he could situate his findings of human sexuality (Gallagher, 2006, p. 5). Just as children turn towards myths for the answers to the riddles of sexuality, Freud turned to the oedipal myth to anchor his theories.

Although the story of Oedipus Rex resonated with Freud as early as 1897, and he could also see the relevance of myths in infantile sexual theories, the connection between the two became prominent to

Freud as he observed Little Hans and his perplexity regarding the birth of his sister, Hanna. In "The sexual enlightenment of children", Freud wrote that the question regarding the origin of babies is also "the oldest and most burning question that confronts immature humanity", and, moreover, "those who understand how to interpret myths and legends" can detect this question in the riddle that the Theban sphinx set for Oedipus (1907c, p. 135). The riddle went as follows: What goes on four feet in the morning, two feet at noon, and three feet in the evening? The answer was: man. This reference to Oedipus is one of the earliest in Freud's work apart from its previous appearance in *Interpretation of Dreams* (1900a, p. 261) and the very first mention of Oedipus Rex in a letter to Fliess dated 15 October 1897 (Masson, 1984). This comment from 1907 illustrates that Freud linked the riddle of the sphinx to the riddle of sexuality for children.

Further, in 1908, Freud again alluded to the myth of Oedipus Rex and connected it to his theories on infantile sexuality, but this time he finds an elusive piece of the theory: castration. The myth of Oedipus Rex in Sophocles' play runs as follows. In short, Oedipus killed his father and married his mother unknowingly. When he realised his deed, he blinded himself and fled the kingdom with his children, while his mother, then his wife, hanged herself.

Freud described that children often obtain pleasure by stimulating the penis with their hands. This is because the early years of childhood are dominated by the excitations originating from the organ. When detected doing so, the child is usually issued with the "threat of castration" by the parents or the primary carers (1908c, p. 217). Freud further added that,

> Legends and myths testify to the upheaval in the child's emotional life and to the horror which is linked with the castration complex – a complex which is subsequently remembered by consciousness with corresponding reluctance. (1908c, p. 217)

Whereas Hans' case was the first discussion of the term, this is the first time Freud mentioned both the concepts "castration complex" and "threat of castration". This comment can be interpreted as follows: (1) the castration complex is associated with the notion of prohibition, and Freud turned towards myths to allude to it; (2) castration is an interruption of socially unacceptable ways of deriving pleasure from the body; (3) if uninterrupted, the enjoyment might lead to future turmoil or disruption such as the fate of Oedipus Rex, who blinded himself; (4) that neurotics subsequently attempt to "forget" this supposed interruption and submit to the demands of the Law, but only *begrudgingly* (see Chapter Seven for more on this point). This is why Freud's intervention in Hans' case involved the installation of a myth which can be interpreted as an attempt to resurrect the real father with the aim of putting an end to the puzzlement about sexual differences. In Freud's theory of castration, it is the real father who issues the threat of castration when the child is faced with the riddles of sexuality: that is, the existential questions of life. These questions are situated at the core of subject formation and their origin is the sexual researches of children.

The following section now elaborates on Freud's use of myth as an intervention in Hans' case. This intervention can be also seen as another missing piece of the puzzle for Freud in formulating the Oedipus complex and developing the theory of the castration complex.

Installing a myth

The treatment of Little Hans was, in fact, in the main conducted via letters to and from the child's father. On one particularly crucial occasion when Freud met Hans in person, he intervened by stating, "Long before he was in the world, I had known that a little Hans would come who would be so fond of his mother that he would be bound to feel afraid of his father because of it; and I told his father this" (1909b, p. 42).

This instance can be interpreted as Freud naming the source of Hans' phobia and offering him an oedipal thread to resolve the phobia, but this was uttered in front of the father and not just to Hans. It is crucial to notice that the installation of this myth was not just aimed at Hans, but was also directed towards Hans' father. Yet, why would we assume so? Verhaeghe suggests that this is not an interpretation but, rather, "is a suggestive construction of something missing", not only for the little boy but also for his father (2000, p. 12, fn. 12). But how? The "missing" bit for Hans could be any of the following: the distinction between the sexes, the knowledge regarding the origin of babies, the reason behind his father *not* intervening, or, even more importantly, the reason behind the physical sensations concerning his "widdler". This eruption of the drive is traumatic and Hans attempted to stop this himself. In Lacanian terms, this was Hans' encounter with the real of the drive, something that cannot be articulated, that escapes symbolisation, and lacked representation. For Verhaeghe, this is the missing piece of the paternal metaphor: a theory that is at the heart of Lacan's Oedipus complex, something that revolves around the father's position. This is why it can be argued that, for Hans' father, the installation of the myth in this instance was a reminder of his function in both his nuclear family and in the wider context of the human race. The function of the father in the family is a difficult concept to grasp for most of the readers of Lacan, let alone the child in the family, and even the fathers themselves.

Very succinctly, the "paternal metaphor" defines the substitutive part of the Oedipus complex for Lacan. The term was introduced by Lacan in 1957, in his Seminar IV, where the case of the Little Hans was elaborated (see Chapter Three for details). A year later, Lacan illustrated the mechanism of this term (Evans, 1996, p. 137). Hence, it is important to highlight the following two points in order to grasp this Lacanian concept: (1) a metaphor is a substitution of one word for another, and (2) the paternal metaphor is, briefly, a mechanism of substitution whereby the enigma of the mother's desire or the desire for the mother is substituted for the name of the father, or the 'No' of the father. The concept of substitution had already been introduced by Freud as the mechanism of condensation in his *Interpretation of Dreams* in 1900. Moreover, Grigg (1999, p. 55) posited that the mechanism of substitution involved in the paternal metaphor is essentially a production of a new meaning, a phallic meaning which introduces the subject to castration. All future signification depends on this fundamental metaphor and, hence, all signification is phallic signification from here on (for details on the relation between paternal metaphor, phallic signification, and castration in Lacan's work, see Chapter Seven).

In the case of the neuroses, this fundamental metaphoric process is repressed, as is evident in Freud's comment from 1908, when he wrote, ". . . subsequently remembered by consciousness with corresponding reluctance" (1908c, p. 217). Whether the mechanism in Hans' case was repression, foreclosure, or disavowal remains a bigger question, the elaboration of which is beyond the scope of this study.

For now, the question is, what purpose was Freud's myth serving in Hans' case? Freud's myth was essentially naming something of the real for Hans, placing it in the symbolic register. Freud's intervention provided a broader view of humans in general by calling upon generations. This was, essentially, an attempt to create a space for Hans in what Lacan calls the symbolic, which would provide him with a view of something beyond the mother. Freud's installation of the myth provided Hans with a broader view of the chain of generation of which he was a part, but was struggling to see any of it beyond his relation with his mother. In other words, Freud's intervention was aimed at pushing Hans from a pre-oedipal stage into the Oedipus complex (pre-oedipal is a Lacanian term, see Chapter Three for elaboration).

It is important to note that the term "Oedipus complex" did not appear until 1910, which was the year after the publication of Hans' case, and that the term "pre-oedipal" is introduced by Lacan in Seminar IV (1956–1957). Therefore, Freud's intervention was aimed at creating an oedipal crisis which subsequently allowed the phobia to reveal itself. In Chapter Six, we learn how the phobia in Hans' case served the function of the father, protecting him from the unbearable real. For now, we can argue that Freud's intervention in Hans's case reveals the following.

To some readers of Freudian theories, it might seem that Freud conceptualises the castrating father as a menacing agent who prohibits the child from desiring the mother. However, his intervention and the installation of myth in this manner in the case of little Hans displays that, to Freud, the father's prohibition is not just aimed at interrupting the child's *guilty* enjoyment (Freud's use of the term). The father's prohibition also *names* that which cannot be articulated by the child without help, particularly the "real" (something that cannot be symbolised) of the drive in the child's body and the father's interruption of it (i.e., castration) also provides the child with a view of something beyond the immediate. If we interpret Freudian conceptualisation of castration in this manner, it highlights how Freud was already discovering the interplay and the differences between the two domains that Lacan was later to formulate as the domains of the imaginary and the symbolic.

Freud's genius is highlighted right here in the case of Little Hans, where he predates modern linguistics and yet captures the mechanisms of metaphor in his intervention. He attempts to substitute the "immediate" of Hans with something "beyond" Hans and his mother that can be captured only in language, something beyond the image. This is an attempt to substitute the imaginary with the symbolic.

The two primary Freudian texts used in this chapter, "The sexual enlightenment of children (An open letter to Dr. M Furst)" (1907c) and "On the sexual theories of children" (1908c) bear witness to Freud's attempt to understand the connection between an adult's sexual life and infantile sexuality. It is evident that the questions of childhood sexual researches are the primitive versions of the existential questions situated at the core of human subjectivity. In particular, questions on the distinction between the sexes and the origin of babies correlate with the questions of one's own existence as a sexed subject; procreation and the act of sex itself are things that language struggles to encompass in their entirety. Freud discovered that, in the researches of children into the matter of sexuality, they turn to myths in order to quench their thirst for knowledge. Freud, too, turned towards a particular myth to help him structure his theories of sexuality: the Oedipus myth.

To sum up, this chapter illustrated that, between 1907 and 1909 for Freud, castration served as a response to the riddles of sexuality in childhood, where the emphasis remained on the absence or presence of the penis and the agent of castration was the real father. In other words, when the child who is ignorant of sexual differences discovers the anatomical differences between the sexes, he assumes that the father must have cut off the girl's penis. For Freud, this is a necessary pathway for the child's entry into what he would later, in 1910, describe as the Oedipus complex (1910h, p. 171). As we shall see in the next chapter. for Freud the Oedipus complex is fundamental to the child's psychosexual development, the formation of his superego, the setting up of his desire for the future (i.e., something beyond the mother), and it is castration that paves the way to this necessary development. This is why Freud would later write that, "castration has already had its effect, which was to force the child into the situation of the Oedipus complex" (1925j, p. 257).

It is becoming evident that the castration complex brings sexual puzzlement to an end and the child begins to notice the difference between the sexes. The next chapter examines the concept of castration for Freud in 1925 and his position in regard to the consequences of the castration complex at that stage by focusing on the text titled

"Some psychical consequences of the anatomical distinction between the sexes" (1925j). In the next chapter, it becomes clearer that it is the Oedipus complex that allows the child to take up a sexual position (Evans, 1996, p. 178) but only when he has accepted castration. For now, we can conclude that the castration complex between 1907 and 1909 was, for Freud, a moment where the infantile theory that "everyone has a penis" is replaced by one where "girls have been castrated" (Evans, 1996, p. 21). Once again, this substitution highlighted by Freud in these texts can be considered as a primitive version of the modern linguistics that Freud clearly predates.

CHAPTER TWO

The castration complex for Freud in 1925

Introduction

During the period between 1907 and 1909, for Freud, the castration complex was enmeshed with infantile sexual researches. By 1925 in Freud's writing, the castration complex was closely linked with the Oedipus complex. The previous chapter examined the inception of the castration complex in Freud's work. This chapter examines Freud's development of the theory of the castration complex in 1925. At this stage, Freud illustrates how the castration complex operates differently in the Oedipus complex for the two sexes. The following papers, dated from 1923–1925, are the best sources for grasping the role of the castration complex within the Oedipus complex. "The infantile genital organization" (1923e) is, essentially, an essay that elaborates the materials presented in Sections 5 and 6 of *Three Essays on the Theory of Sexuality* (1905d) which, as illustrated in Chapter One, had its origin in the 1907 and the 1908 papers (1907c and 1908c). "The dissolution of the Oedipus complex" (1924d) is where, for the first time, the difference between the sexual development of boys and girls was emphasised, and "Some psychical consequences of the anatomical distinction between the sexes" (1925j), according to

Strachey, is "the first complete re-assessment of Freud's views on the psychological development of women" (1925j, pp. 243–258). It is on this text (previously titled "Anatomical sex-distinction") that this chapter focuses in order to examine Freud's position regarding the castration complex in 1925 and to highlight the consequences of the castration complex in boys and girls. The aim of this chapter is not just to provide a close reading of the text itself with a view to examining the above, but, considering that Freud makes various references in these texts to many other texts of his own (such as his frequent use of footnotes), the chapter is purposely designed in a manner that would make other immediate references related to the text available and accessible to readers, allowing them to read these in a single chapter.

Situating Freud

Before discussing the 1925 text, it is important to highlight some of the comments that capture Freud's position around the 1920s on the question of castration. As mentioned before, it it is in the year 1920 that Freud suggested that there existed certain masculine and feminine psychical characteristics that are impossible to define in "The psychogenesis of a case of homosexuality in a woman" (1920a, p. 171). The following remark truly captures Freud's position in terms of the sexual characteristics of human beings and it remains so throughout his career.

> ... psychoanalysis can not elucidate the intrinsic nature of what in conventional and biological phraseology is termed "masculine" and "feminine": it simply takes over the two concepts and makes them the foundation of its work. When we attempt to reduce them further, we find masculinity vanishing into activity and femininity into passivity, and that does not tell us enough. (1920a, p. 171)

At the beginning of life, the human subject is ignorant of sexual differences (1923e, p. 145). In "The infantile genital organization", Freud explained that in the "pre-genital sadistic–anal organization" stage, there is "no question of male or female" (1923e, p. 145). They begin to acquire these psychical characteristics at the stage of the "infantile genital organization" through complex psychical processes where "anatomical differences interact with social and psychical factors" (Evans, 1996, p. 178). However, these processes are neither "natural" nor "made", that is, constructed. The cultural imperative and the imposition of cultural norms indicate that sexuality is not "natural" but is a cultural phenomena, something constructed within the context of the culture. However, such a perception of sexuality lacks the subjective thread that makes sexuality a matter of individuality. For Freud, these processes of the formation of sexuality are grounded on the theories of *Trieb*. The question of sexual differences for Freud in the early 1920s revolves around the castration complex and with Freud's emphasis remaining on the real male organ, the penis.

"The infantile genital organization" is an extremely crucial text in understanding how Freud built his argument with regard to the pivotal role of the castration complex within the Oedipus complex. It is in this text where Freud illustrated clearly that the effect of castration has a close relation with the perception of the feminine genital. Freud wrote, "the lack of a penis is regarded as a result of castration, and so now the child is faced with the task of coming to terms with castration in relation to himself" (1923e, p. 144). In other words, Freud iterated that the knowledge of the anatomical differences is essential for the child to recognise the power of the threat of castration (i.e., the power of the castrating father). The recognition of this difference between the sexes with regard to power helps the child to recognise the difference between the sexes (the first puzzle of childhood researches) but not just anatomical differences, something more, because it is only when he begins to recognise a power beyond himself, and beyond his mother, that the child faces the question of castration in relation to himself. Freud's emphasis on the penis in the castration complex remained since its inception, as discussed in the previous chapter. Hence, the central theme of the castration complex for Freud in 1923 is an "antithesis . . . between having a *male genital* and being *castrated*" (1923e, p. 145). When his fellow theorists and colleagues suggested that the castration complex could be conceptualised as parallel to the phenomena of weaning (loss of breast) or the birthing experience itself (loss of the protection of the womb), Freud maintained his position and insisted in 1923 that "the term 'castration complex' ought to be confined to those excitations and consequences which are bound up with the loss of the *penis*" (1909b, p. 8, fn. 2). This comment was added as a footnote in 1923 to Hans' case history, titled *Analysis of a Phobia in a Five-year-old-Boy* (1909b). A similar position is also expressed in the following comment, made in 1923 in "The infantile genital organization" (1923e). Freud wrote, *"the significance of the castration complex can only be rightly appreciated if its origin in the phase of phallic primacy is also taken into account"* (1923e, p. 144).

The emphasis on the term "phallic" was highlighted in the following fashion at this stage of Freud's writing. Freud considered that the significance of the castration complex lies in the phallic stage because it "is not a primacy of the genitals, but a primacy of the *phallus*" (1923e, p. 142). It can be concluded, then, that, in the 1920s, for Freud, in both sexes the object of castration is the phallus and the significance of the phallus is equal for both at the phallic stage. It is this emphasis on the phallus that would open up new avenues for Freud to speculate about the theories of the castration complex in 1925, as we shall see in the close reading of "Some psychical consequences of the anatomical distinction between the sexes", below.

The term "phallus" is also significant for Lacan, who reformulated Freudian theories and announced that the phallus is a signifier for desire (see Chapter Seven). However, Freud did not abandon his theories regarding the organ, the penis. He continued to assert that the child assumes that, in girls, "the lack of penis is the result of having been castrated as a punishment", but this time Freud added that the boy believes that only the "unworthy" females who gave in to their impulses, like himself, lost their penises (1923e, p. 144). This would suggest that children might consider that females who *are worthy* do possess a penis. This will become an important piece of information later in the formulation of theories of "phallic women" (see Chapters Four, Five, and Six).

Freud also confirmed that ". . . the destruction of the Oedipus complex is brought about by the threat of castration" (1924d, p. 177), because seeing "a creature . . . so like himself . . . the loss of his penis becomes imaginable" to the child (1924d, p. 178). Freud highlighted the difference between the sexes as ". . . the girl accepts castration as an accomplished fact, whereas the boy fears the possibility of its occurrence" (1924d, p. 178). But, soon after this declaration, Freud admitted that ". . . in general our insight into these developmental processes in girls is unsatisfactory, incomplete and vague" (1924d, p. 179). The most important element from these texts and quotations from the early 1920s that contain Freud's formulation of a universal theory of psychosexual development is his determination to provide two distinct sets of developmental theory for the two sexes and his own puzzlement about feminine sexuality. In the Editor's note, Strachey wrote that ". . . the problem of the sexual history of women was no doubt constantly in Freud's mind" (1925j, p. 245). However, the "problem" did not stop Freud from acknowledging his own limits or from continuing to postulate.

The concept of bisexuality and the active–passive drive

Freud speaks about the concepts of bisexuality and the notion of the active–passive drive in the text titled, "Some psychical consequences of the anatomical distinction between the sexes" (1925j). However, it is important to remember that these concepts were already mentioned in *Three Essays on the Theory of Sexuality* (1905d) and also that these concepts have been speculated about throughout Freud's other work at various stages of his career. According to Strachey, in a footnote to *The Ego and the Id* (1923b, p. 33, fn. 1), the earliest mention of bisexuality in Freud's work was in a letter to Fliess, recorded as Letter 113, dated 1 August 1899. Three of those instances are crucial in relation to this current text.

1.   In 1915, Freud added a footnote to *Three Essays on the Theory of Sexuality* acknowledging that he regarded bisexuality as a decisive factor and an essential concept without which it is impossible to understand the sexual manifestations in both men and women (1905d, p. 220, fn. 1).
2.   In 1915, Freud highlighted that the concepts of "masculine" and "feminine" are best understood in psychoanalysis as corresponding with activity and passivity of the drive. In this sense, when libido has an aim, even if it is a passive aim, it is to be considered as masculine, because the drive is always active (1905d, p. 220, fn. 1). This raises a further question as to whether a drive without aim is to be considered as feminine. Moreover, in regard to the sociological meaning of the terms "masculine" and "feminine", Freud added that every human displays a mixture of characteristics belonging to both sexes and "shows a combination of activity and

passivity whether or not these last character-traits tally with his biological ones" (1905d, p. 220, fn. 1).

3.   In 1923, in *The Ego and the Id*, Freud suggested that, due to bisexuality, which is originally present in children, "the more complete Oedipus complex" is "twofold", as it consists of "positive and negative" outcomes (1923b, p. 33). For example, consider a boy who has an ambivalent attitude towards his father and considers his mother as his object of affection. According to Freud, at the same time, this boy might also behave like a girl by displaying a feminine affectionate attitude towards his father while feeling jealousy and hostility towards his mother. The element of bisexuality, thus, muddles the connection between identification and object choices (1923b, p. 33). Last, it would be useful to quote Freud from *Three Essays on the Theory of Sexuality* (1905d) on this particular subject before engaging with his text from 1925 on the same subject (see Chapter Four for further discussion on bisexuality and drive). In a section titled "The differentiation between men and women", Freud wrote,

> Indeed, if we were able to give a more definite connotation to the concepts of "masculine" and "feminine", it would even be possible maintain that libido is invariably and necessarily of a masculine nature, whether it occurs in men or in women and irrespectively of whether its object is a man or a woman. (1905d, p. 219)

"Some psychical consequences of the anatomical distinction between the sexes" (Freud 1925j)

"Whereas in boys the Oedipus complex is destroyed by the castration complex, in girls it is made possible and led up to by the castration complex" (Freud, 1925j, p. 256).

Freud began by highlighting the difficulties of formulating a straightforward theory of the Oedipus complex for boys. He explained that, for a boy at the first stage of the Oedipus complex, his libido, which is "not as yet a genital one", is invested in his first object, the mother. The boy considers his father as "a disturbing rival and would like to get rid of him and take his place" (1925j, p. 250). This oedipal attitude belongs to the phallic phase and, due to the boy's narcissistic investment in his penis, the threat of castration triggers the destruction of the Oedipus complex. Yet, there are multiple complexities that get in the way of formulating a straightforward theory of the boy's psychosexual development. Much of Freud's postulations and theories presented here are derived from his clinical observations, especially from the case study of the Wolf-man. Considering the depth, importance, and complexity of the Wolf-man case history (1918b), and further mentions of this case history at various stages of Freud's writing, the following will restrict itself to the findings highlighted in this particular paper from 1925. The focus will remain on Freud's theorisation of the castration complex and its role in the Oedipus complex, as illustrated in this Freudian text only.

In line with the "bisexual constitution", Freud noted that "the Oedipus complex has a double orientation, active and passive" (1925j, p. 250). The term "feminine attitude", for Freud in 1925, referred to the phenomenon of the boy wishing to take his mother's place and choosing his father as the "love-object" (1925j, p. 250). This passive position, however, does not present itself without the possibility of losing his penis; that is, the threat of castration is also evident in this position. This is because, in his limited knowledge of sexual matters, the child understands that choosing the feminine position in sexual acts as his mother would also entail losing his penis as a precondition to femininity. Nevertheless, it is a complication that stands in the way of developing a universal clear-cut theory of the Oedipus complex in boys.

Moreover, Freud highlighted that the pre-history of the boy's Oedipus complex raised further questions. For instance, the boy's affectionate identification with his father might not include rivalry with his mother. Freud also assumed that infantile "masturbation is attached to the Oedipus complex and serves as a discharge for the sexual excitation belonging to it" (1925j, p. 250). The threat of castration is usually issued by the primary carers with regard to the child's infantile masturbatory habits. These habits might include his interest in his genital (touching the organ with his hands) but also could include his habit of bed-wetting. The phenomenon of bed-wetting can, thus, be seen as a result of the child's effort to suppress his genital activity, "that is, as having the meaning of a threat of castration" (1925j, p. 250). Furthermore, particularly from the analysis of the Wolf-man, Freud suggested that ". . . a child at a very early age listening to his parents copulating may set up his first sexual excitation" and this event, "owing to its after-effects", might "act as a starting-point for the child's whole sexual development" (1925j, p. 250). In the case of the Wolf-man, Freud illustrated how the child interpreted the meaning of this accidental sight or sound of his parents copulating. In his case, the question of masturbation and the active–passive attitudes of the Oedipus complex became attached to the Wolf-man's early experience of witnessing parental copulation. However, Freud accepted that it is impossible to consider such a consequence as a universal one and, hence, the problem of "primal phantasies" would be considered as another obstacle in formulating the theory of Oedipus complex in boys (1925j, p. 251).

Freud believed that, for both the boy and the girl, the mother is the original object in the Oedipus complex but he wanted to investigate the process of how the girl abandons the mother and chooses her father as the object instead. From clinical experiences, Freud noticed a wishful phantasy in women of having a child by the father. This phantasy might also be considered as the motive force behind girls' infantile masturbation. Freud suggested that, for girls, "the Oedipus complex has a long pre-history and is in some respects a secondary formation" (1925j, p. 251). When little girls accidentally discover the penis of a playmate or a brother, they notice the "strikingly visible" difference, recognise "it as the superior counterpart of their own small and inconspicuous organ, and from that time forward fall a victim to envy for the penis" (1925j, p. 252).

Disavowal–denial, Leugnen–Verleugnen

Freud noted that, at the first sight of the girl's genital area, the boy shows a "lack of interest", as if he has seen nothing; he disavows it (1925j, p. 252). The name for this concept used by Freud in 1923 was *leugnen*, but, in 1924 and in this present text, according to Strachey, the term becomes *Verleugnen*. When used in relation to the castration complex, the term, for Freud, meant "denial" or "to deny". This is not being equated with *Verneinen*, which means "negation" (1925h, p. 143). This disavowal emerges due to the boy's refusal to submit to the threat of castration. Which is why only when, later, the threat obtains a hold upon him, the boy experiences emotional turmoil and is forced "to believe in the reality of the threat" which previously he had laughed at (1925j, p. 252). The circumstances lead to two reactions which, combined with other factors or on their own, "permanently determine the boy's relation to women: horror of the mutilated creature or triumphant contempt for her" (1925j, p. 252). Such revision of past events and (not of lived experiences) at a later date is a fundamental concept in Freudian theories known as the deferred effect (*nactraglichkeit*) and it is evident both in the Little Hans case and the Wolf-man case history. It was Lacan who drew attention to the importance of this concept later; however, it is beyond both the aim and scope of this book to provide more details on this concept.

The little girl, on the other hand, makes her judgement and decision "in a flash", as Freud argued that "she has seen it and knows that she is without it and wants to have it" (1925j, p. 252). At this stage in the text, Freud recalled his previous conclusion regarding the order of the childhood sexual research questions from 1908 and corrected himself. Previously, he stated that it was the origin of babies and not the question regarding the difference between the sexes that aroused sexual interest in children. Now, he states that it is certainly not the case for girls "at all events" and for boys might be true in some cases (1925j, p. 252). This is because, from later clinical observations, Freud learnt that it is the riddle of the difference between the sexes that leads to the future formation of the masculinity complex in women. The development of femininity might be affected by this "branching off". The hope of someday acquiring a penis and becoming a man might persist until a surprisingly late age and it might also be the reason for "strange and otherwise unaccountable actions" (1925j, p. 253). Or else, the woman might disavow and refuse to accept that she has been castrated and "behave as though she were a man", believing that she does possess a penis (1925j, p. 253). In other words, there are "various and far-reaching" psychical consequences for the girl when she discovers the anatomical difference between the sexes, but the two major ones are penis envy and the reaction formation of the masculinity complex (1925j, p. 253). Freud explains that the knowledge of the anatomical difference is a "wound to her narcissism" and, like a "scar", she develops "a sense of inferiority" (1925j, p. 253), but after the stage where she realises that her lack is not just a personal punishment but a universal sexual characteristic, "she shares the contempt felt by men" and "insists on being like a man" (1925j, p. 253).

Jealousy

Penis envy continues to exist even after it "has abandoned its true object", the penis, in the form of jealousy (1925j, p. 254). Freud connected this character trait that, according to him, is commonly found in women with another common occurrence in girls, which is also a "relic of the phallic period in girls": the phantasy of "a child is being beaten" (1925j, p. 254). This is a reference to his paper of the same title published in 1919 (1919e). He concluded that the beating can be interpreted as caressing of the clitoris, as the child in the phantasy represents the clitoris. The revelation of the phantasy is, thus, "a confession of masturbation" (1925j, p. 254). The girl could also show jealousy of another child, believing that her mother is "fonder" of the other child than of her. For Freud, this can be seen as the child's contempt for her mother. Since it was the mother who had brought the little girl into this world "so insufficiently equipped", she holds the mother responsible for her "lack of a penis" (1925j, p. 254). This gives her the necessary reason for giving up her mother as the first object-choice. This theory also fits if the child in the beating phantasy *is* the child whom the girl feels her mother is fonder of than herself.

Clitoral masturbation

Penis envy, for Freud in this text, is a synonym for "the discovery of the inferiority of the clitoris" (1925j, p. 254). While every individual human, irrespective of his or her anatomical sex, is "made up of masculine and feminine traits", Freud wondered why it is that, compared to men, masturbation seems further removed from the nature of women (1925j, p. 254). Freud concluded that masturbation is a masculine activity, even when it concerns the clitoris, "and that the elimination of the clitoral sexuality is a necessary precondition for the development of femininity" (1925j, p. 255). We can assume that, since libido is always masculine for Freud because it always has an aim, the expression of masturbation logically seems masculine to Freud for both men and women. From clinical observation, Freud concluded that, after the first sign of penis envy, girls experience intense emotion, an "intense current of feeling" that forces them "against masturbation" (1925j, p. 255). This "current" can be interpreted as a prelude to repression that deals with the girl's pubertal expression of her massive masculine sexuality and, thus, makes the necessary "room for the development of her femininity" (1925j, p. 255). Drawing from his clinical observations, Freud also concluded that girls, too, could be struggling to free themselves from the "compulsion to masturbate" (1925j, p. 255). What are the manifestations of this compulsion? Freud proposes that women's struggle against the compulsion to masturbate could be responsible for several later "manifestations of sexual life in women" which are, and will remain, "unintelligible" unless "this powerful motive is recognized" (1925j, p. 255). The "recognition of the anatomical distinction between the sexes" is, thus, in girls, seen as a phenomenon that "forces her away from masculinity, masculine masturbation", and leads her to the new path of "the development of femininity", according to Freud (1925j, p. 255).

It is worth pausing to reflect upon a few viewpoints that have emerged so far. Apart from the feminists' arguments and demands for equal rights and Freud's provocative choice of words, which do not seem friendly at times in describing the female body and feminine psychical reactions, there is a lot more worth highlighting here. The immediate questions that arise are as follows.

1. In this particular text, it appears that, for Freud, the recognition of anatomical distinction between the sexes and the castration threat by the father are central to the notion of castration.

2. Strachey suggested that the term "disavowal", which also has a verb form ("disavow"), implying an action, is often used in Freudian texts in relation to the castration complex. In this particular text, "disavowal" appears to be one of the psychical consequences of the recognition of the anatomical differences between the sexes and also as a reaction to the father's castrating threat. Following this line of thought, it appears that Freudian theory, here, is indicating that masculine masturbation and masculinity in women is to be interpreted as the girl disavowing castration.

3. Freud uses the term "disavow" in relation to the question of "fetishism" at several stages of his career, but not in this text from 1925. Although Freud uses masculine pronouns (he/him) in such instances where he connects the two terms, it is clear, none the less, that, for Freud, the fetishist disavows "his own sense-perception . . . that the female genitals lack a penis" (1940a,

p. 202). Based on this later connection that Freud makes between "disavow" and "fetishism", one could ask, are cases where women are not "feminine" in the Freudian sense (which is not yet clear) to be considered as cases of fetishism? This question emerges because, in this 1925 text, Freud has described the concept of disavowal in a woman as her insistence that she does, indeed, possess a penis. Freud has clearly outlined in this paper that such a perception of hers might find its expression in the form of her indulgence in clitoral masturbation, or her attachment to her masculinity complex, or she might also consider her child as the lost penis. This is a question of feminine fetishism and its relation to the Freudian theorisation of castration which deserves further investigation.

4.   In relation to the Freudian theory of fetishism, Hans' "widdler" confusion and his mother's affirmation that she does possess a penis (widdler) raise the question of both the child's and the mother's disavowal of castration. Perhaps, it was the strength of Hans' infantile impulse that did not take the usual route of repression and Hans remained attached "to the person of his primitive object-choice", or, perhaps, like most neurotics, Hans' mother was unable to answer the question asked by her child in relation to sex. Either way, in this 1925 text, it remained a question concerning the role of the father as the issuer of the threat of castration. A Lacanian perspective of this matter is provided in the next chapter.

5.   Finally, there is no mention of the vagina in this current text, apart from the "horror" that the boy experiences in the perception of the absence of the penis in girls.

However, Freud's puzzlement over the enigma of femininity, his struggle to define and theorise the development of femininity, his determination and openness regarding the subject matter reflect his genius and, most of all, his human-ness. For, as is illustrated in the first chapter, "What is a woman?" is a fundamental question for every neurotic. It is essential to acknowledge that, although Lacan's development of Freudian theories around sexual difference and, in particular, the question of femininity contributes immensely, it is beyond the scope of this book to include them here.

Penis-child: the girl has turned into a little woman

The question that Freud asked at the beginning of this text was, "how does it happen that girls abandon it [the mother as the object] and instead take their father as an object?" (1925j, p. 251). Freud's answer to the question at this point in the text is as follows. All the above consequences of penis envy are to be considered as phenomena leading the girl to her Oedipus complex. Those consequences are *not* her Oedipus complex and the complex *did not* play any part in those consequences. It can be added that, in this case, it was the castration complex that played the crucial part here because it was the recognition of anatomical difference that led to the girl's penis envy in the first place and, hence, we can argue that such recognition is synonymous with the theory of castration. The girl's libido, at this stage, aligns itself to a new position: the "penis-child" (1925j, p.256). She gives up her wish for a penis and replaces it with the "wish for a child: and *with that purpose in view*, she takes her father as a love-object" (1925j, p. 256). As a result of the displacement of her penis envy, the girl's mother subsequently becomes the object of her jealousy. As the child transforms into a "little woman", Freud suggested that she might also experience physical sensations, which are to be regarded as a "premature awakening of the female genital apparatus" (1925j, p. 256). However, later on, if the girl's attachment to her father comes to a halt, she might abandon him as an object and begin to identify with him. Thus, her masculinity complex could return in future and the girl might remain "fixated in it" (1925j, p. 256).

Thus, the quote that opened the close reading in this chapter is a summary of the following. While most of this Freudian text served the much-needed purpose of shedding some light on the girl's Oedipus complex, the boy's complex remains "more or less unknown" (1925j, p. 256). The phenomenon of penis envy and its consequences described here are to be considered as "the operations of the castration complex" in girls (1925j, p. 256). In that sense, the castration complex in girls prepares them for their entry into the Oedipus complex and, thus, in girls, the Oedipus complex is to be interpreted as a secondary formation, whereas, in boys, the castration complex smashes their Oedipus complex. This *is* the fundamental contrast between the sexes for Freud in 1925. This contradiction is also in line with Freud's rationale. Indeed, for Freud, castration operates in the same manner as the name suggests, "it inhibits and limits masculinity and encourages femininity" (1925j, p. 256).

The difference between girls' and boys' sexual development discussed in this text is, hence, a "consequence of the anatomical distinction between their genitals and the psychical situation involved in it" (1925j, p. 257). The difference lies "between a castration that has been carried out", which is the case of the boys, "and one that has merely been threatened", that is the case of the girls (1925j, p. 257). The manner in which the child enters and leaves the stage of the Oedipus complex will have significant impact on his and her future development. For boys, the Oedipus complex is not just repressed, but, rather, "it is literally smashed to pieces by the shock of threatened castration" (1925j, p. 257). This means that castration in boys is an essential phenomenon which allows further developments to take place, such as, castration forces the boy to abandon the oedipal "libidinal cathexes" and it sexualises and partly sublimates the boy's Oedipal libido (1925j, p. 257). Subsequently, the ego incorporates the objects of the Oedipus complex and, thus, the formation of the superego begins to take place in the boy. This formulation is responsible for the boy's structure (in the Lacanian sense of the term) and his characteristics. Please note that "structure" is not a Freudian term, but, in this sentence, it provides the sense of "organisation" or "organising". In Freudian terms, it can be concluded that, in "ideal cases", the Oedipus complex does not exist any longer, not even in the unconscious, and the superego becomes "its heir" (1925j, p. 257). This will lead us to assume that the negotiation of the Oedipus complex has not really been completed in females within the context of Freud's theories discussed in this chapter.

Neurosis: a struggle of the ego against the demands of the sexual function (1925j, p. 257)

Freud believes that the motive for the "demolition of the Oedipus complex" is evident in boys but lacking in girls (1925j, p. 257). The boy would become a man and, perhaps, a father only when he leaves his parental nest and builds his own. However, to gain the promise of the future he must give up his enjoyment of the present. In this regard, it can be added that Hans was caught up in the riddles of the difference between the sexes, the origin of babies, and, moreover, he was caught up in his bodily enjoyment, of which he was unable to make sense. Hans was also enmeshed in the dynamics of the marital couple, his parents. As Lacan puts it, Hans became his mother's little appendage, the little husband. In this sense, Hans also became the symptom of the couple. Faced with the questions of sexuality and the sensation originating in his organ, Hans was confronted with the real in the Lacanian sense. His enjoyment had an element of this real, that Lacan would later coin as *jouissance*. For Freud, this is a struggle (as reflected in the above quote), where the boy's ego usually wins. As Freud emphasises, the boy has to (1) accept the possibility of castration, and (2) recognise that women are castrated. This is further illustrated in the following extract.

> The penis (to follow Ferenczi [1924]) owes its extraordinarily high narcissistic cathexis to its organic significance for the propagation of the species, the catastrophe to the Oedipus complex (the abandonment of incest and the institution of conscience and morality) may be regarded as a victory of the race over the individual. (Freud, 1925j, p. 257)

Consider the above statement, ". . . the abandonment of incest and the institution of conscience and morality" and compare it to Freud's comment made in 1907 in relation to Hans, "*not having been intimidated or oppressed with a sense of guilt*, he gives expression quite ingenuously to what he thinks" (1907c, p. 135, my italics). The former comment, from 1925, now appears as a more developed and concrete version of the latter. Hans was, indeed, in urgent need of an intervention that would not only force him to abandon his incestuous wishes but also would install "the institution of conscience and morality" in him. The comment also paves the way for Freud's intervention, as discussed in the previous chapter. Similar to the riddle of the sphinx, a larger view of humankind was installed in Freud's intervention (see Chapter One).

However, compared to the boy, in the girl's case, since there is no such *clear motive* for the destruction of the Oedipus complex, there is no *clear pathway* for the destruction of the complex. The girl can abandon the complex slowly; she can also repress it, or the effects of the complex might persist in future and it might have an impact on her "normal mental life" (1925j, p. 257). This ambiguity about the woman's negotiation of the Oedipus complex, the mere fact that the threat of castration does not "shatter" her Oedipus complex, and her lack of motive to submit to the paternal law, led Freud to utter the following, with some hesitation, ". . . for women the level of what is ethically normal is different from what is in men" (1925j, p. 257). Her superego is "inexorable", "impersonal", and "independent of its emotional origins as we require it to be in men" (1925j, p. 257). In other words, Freud alluded to having an *a priori* concept that the propagation of the species requires a set of morals to be in place among humans, which the woman lacks. Freud continues to speculate that women's "sense of justice" is less than that of men, she is rather "less ready to submit to the great exigencies of life" (1925j, p. 258). It is "the modification in the formation of her super-ego" that can be held responsible for her apparent unclear judgement, which is more often influenced "by feelings of affection or hostility" (1925j, p. 258).

These moments are important to keep in mind, as they will be revisited in Chapters Three and Five when we examine Freud's reformulation of the theories on feminine sexuality and its relation to castration. In particular, the formation of the woman's superego and her hostility is important for the discussion in the later chapters. Yet, soon after this comment, acknowledging the anxious feminist readers, Freud concluded that it is not solely women who fail to completely achieve the position of the ideal femininity. In fact, the majority of men are "far behind the masculine ideal" (1925j, p. 258). Rather, he emphasised that all humans possess both masculine and feminine character traits due to "their bisexual disposition" and "cross-inheritance" (1925j, p. 258). This notion of the bisexual disposition is revisited in the coming chapters, but, for now, Freud acknowledges that, due to the presence of the bisexual disposition in both sexes, the concepts of "pure" masculinity and femininity will "remain theoretical constructions of uncertain content" (1925j, p. 258).

With the addition of this comment, it can be concluded that Freud returned to the two notions, bisexuality and the active–passive drive, with which he began this 1925 text. On the one hand, these two concepts gave rise to complications and obstacles in the pathway of formulating the theory of the Oedipus complex for boys. On the other hand, it is these two concepts that enabled Freud to smooth out the theory of the girl's Oedipus complex. In the future, do these two concepts help Freud in formulating further theories on sexuality?

To sum up, this chapter illustrates that, in 1925, for Freud, the castration complex was enmeshed with the Oedipus complex. Here, Freud further developed his previous theories of childhood sexual researches and considered the recognition of the anatomical difference between the sexes as castration. This chapter also highlighted the effects of castration as it emerged in this particular text, titled, "Some psychical consequences of the anatomical distinction between the sexes" (1925j).

Castration plays different roles in boys and girls. For Freud, the emphasis, however, remains in the phallic stage for both the sexes. Unless the threat of castration emerges and is recognised, the boy cannot enter the stage of the Oedipus complex, whereas, for girls, castration leads them up to the Oedipus complex. The fate of both depends on their individual negotiation of the complex. Whereas, for boys, Freud has provided theoretical suppositions of what might be the outcome in general of their negotiation of the Oedipus complex, in girls, the matter remains open for further discussion. Boys have a clear motive for their Oedipus complex being not only repressed, but shattered, but girls lack such a clear motive to destroy their Oedipus complex. This leaves a question mark around the development of the girl's superego, responsible for her sense of justice. Moreover, the phenomenon of disavowing the anatomical distinction between sexes seems to equate with the concept of disavowing castration. Importantly, however, it is evident that both the boy and the girl may disavow.

CHAPTER THREE

Freud's theories of castration in "Female sexuality" (1931b)

Introduction

C hapter One has already illustrated that, for Freud, the riddle of sexuality in childhood sexual researches comes to an end with the discovery of the anatomical differences. This discovery was synonymous with the concept of castration complex for Freud between 1907 and 1909. Chapter Two examined Freud's 1925 text and we learnt that the discovery of sexual differences have different consequences in the psyches of the boy and the girl. In other words, we examined Freud's theories on the psychical consequences of castration as described in 1925. In this chapter, we try to understand how Freud conceptualised the little girl's negotiation of the riddles of sexuality in the 1930s. According to Grigg (1999) and Strachey's editorial note to "The infantile genital organization" (1923e), "The dissolution of the Oedipus complex" (1924d), and "Some psychical consequences of the anatomical distinction between the sexes" (1925j) are three of Freud's important contributions that sparked off a heated debate in the psychoanalytic circle between the 1920s and 1930s on the question of female sexuality. Known as the Freud–Jones debate, it not only revolved around the question of what constitutes femininity and its relation to the phallus, or the phallic stage, as Freud articulated in the above mentioned texts from 1923 and 1924, but also heated discussion took place on the question of object-relation, particularly that of the mother and the child. Two of the most controversial proposals of Freud that influenced the great debate on female sexuality were (1) that there is only one libido and that is masculine, even in the case of the little girl, and (2) that, for Freud, female psychosexual development is all about how "a woman develops out of a child with a bi-sexual disposition" (1933a, p. 116). While the first proposal seems to be the primary topic in "Female sexuality" (1931b), the second text, "Femininity" (1933a, Lecture XXXIII, pp. 112–135) seems to be focusing more on Freud's second proposal.

One of the ripple effects of this debate was that it influenced Freud's style of investigation of the feminine psychosexual development and he reformulated his theories of the feminine in the early 1930s. Instead of continuing on his previous line of questioning, which revolved around the effects and the outcomes of the Oedipus complex in the little girl, Freud's investigation in these texts focused on the little girl's entry into the Oedipus complex. This emphasis of Freud's on the making of the woman, not what she becomes or might become, but, rather, how she came to be is of particular interest here: "... psychoanalysis does not try to describe what a woman is ... but sets about how she comes into being ..." (Freud, 1933a, p. 116). This line of questioning is different than that of biology, anatomy, and physiology. Such a position of Freud's is also reflected in his comment, "... we must keep psychoanalysis separate from biology just as we have kept it from anatomy and physiology" (Freud, 1971[1935]). Since such shifts were most evident in his texts titled "Female sexuality" (1931b) and "Femininity" (1933a, Lecture XXXIII), these two texts are invaluable in understanding how Freud formulated the theory of female sexuality in relation to the theory of castration in the 1930s. I have provided close readings of both these texts.

This chapter focuses only on "Female sexuality" (1931b) and Chapter Five will explore "Femininity" (1933a, Lecture XXXIII). The structure of the close reading will allow the readers to follow how Freud built his arguments. There is repetition at times, similar to the way there is repetition in Freud's text. These repetitions allow the readers to appreciate the complexity and difficulty Freud experienced in defining the theory of female psychosexual development in relation to his theories on castration.

From the text titled "Female sexuality" (1931b)

According to the oedipal theory that Freud has proposed during the 1920s, both the little boy and the little girl experience hostility towards the parent of the same sex and love for the opposite sex "during the phase of the normal Oedipal complex" (1931b, p. 225). Here, "normal" can be interpreted as referring to cases where the child's future psychosexual development remains comparatively less troubling than those whose psychopathologies are rather difficult to contain and require intervention. The term "normal" becomes more comprehensible if we were to remind ourselves that, in psychoanalysis, there is no cure for the "human condition" and the difference in psychopathologies is usually referred to as difference in degrees and not in kind. Moreover, a "normal Oedipus complex" can be also be regarded as a reference to Freud's previous passing comment about the "positive" outcome of the Oedipus complex (1923b, p. 33), where the child develops a heterosexual infantile attachment with regard to his parent of the opposite sex. The latter is of importance here. Considering that, in the case of both the little boy and the little girl, the mother is the first "love-object", the boy's oedipal attachment to his mother and his rivalry towards his father is not difficult to understand. However, the question of the little girl's Oedipus complex is not so clear. Freud highlighted two aspects for further examination: (1) the way the girl turns away from her first love-object (her mother) and chooses her father as her love-object remains unclear, and (2) how she gives up on her previous "leading genital zone" the clitoris and begins to favour the vagina (1931b, p. 225). In the case of the little girl, Freud proposed that the two most prominent changes that influence the development of her femininity are: (1) the abandonment of her previous clitoral enjoyment and favouring the vagina as the new leading genital zone and (2) "the exchange of her original object – her mother – for her father" (p. 225).

Based on his clinical practice and observation of women who displayed strong attachment to their father, Freud was struck by two new aspects of female sexuality. First, Freud noted that analysis with such women revealed that their strong and intense attachment to their father usually came after "a phase of exclusive attachment" to the mother, which was "equally intense and passionate" (p. 225), meaning that the little girl's primary attachment to her mother is rich and multi-dimensional. Second, Freud was struck by the duration of this early attachment which, although varied (in some cases it lasted until the fifth year), it mostly covered the longest period of the "early sexual efflorescence" (p. 226). Hence, there is a possibility that some women remain caught in their original attachment to their mother and do not quite accomplish "a true change-over towards men" (p. 226). It is based on these observations that Freud highlighted the importance of the pre-oedipal stage for women. Although the Oedipus complex is considered the "nucleus of the neuroses" and adult psychopathologies can be traced back to the subject's oedipal stage, for females, however, the case is different (p. 226). It is only after the initial "negative complex" that a girl reaches the "normal positive Oedipus situation" (p. 226). Which means that during the pre-oedipal stage the little girl does experience her father as the "troublesome rival". The question is, then, how does the little girl change her love-object and enter the "normal positive Oedipus situation", or, rather, does she do this at all?

It is essential to note that Freud, in *The Ego and the Id* (1923b, p. 33), passingly described the Oedipus complex as "two-fold" due to the presence of bisexuality in children. In the case of the little girl, the "normal positive Oedipus situation" is where she experiences hostility towards her mother and chooses her father as her love object and the opposite is referred to as a "negative complex" (1931b, p. 226). However, it would be misleading to assume that there is any such clear-cut distinction and Freud has warned his readers against these assumptions repeatedly. The presence of this complicated element called bisexuality "makes it so difficult to obtain a clear view of the facts in connection with the earliest object-choices and identifications, and still more difficult to describe them intelligibly" (Freud, 1923b, p. 33).

Also important to note here is that the concept called the "negative Oedipus complex" is supported by the Dutch doctor and psychoanalyst, Jeanne Lampl-de Groot (1928, pp. 332–345). She agrees with Freud's view that, prior to the girl's entry into the Oedipus complex, during the pre-oedipal phase, the little girl is in a negative Oedipus situation (Grigg, 1999, p. 167). However, Freud disagrees with Lampl-de Groot on the grounds that she does not emphasise enough the element of hostility involved in the girl's turning away from her mother, which has crucial clinical implications (Freud, 1931b, p. 241). This particular point is further elaborated in the coming sections. For now, to assume that there is "a neat parallelism between male and female sexual development" would be another mistake (Freud, 1931b, p. 226). Freud's discovery of the importance of the little girl's pre-oedipal phase supports this statement.

If we remind ourselves of a particular comment Freud made in "Some psychical consequences of the anatomical distinction between the jusexes" (1925j), we can begin to grasp the connection between female sexuality and castration complex. Freud noted, "*Whereas in boys the Oedipus complex is destroyed by the castration complex, in girls it is made possible and led up to by the castration complex*" (1925j, p. 256). In other words, it is the castration complex that leads the little girl up to her Oedipus complex and it is the castration complex that makes the little girl's Oedipus complex possible. Which means that the little girl's pre-oedipal stage *is* where she is beginning to be affected by the castration complex. The emphasis Freud places on the knowledge of the little girl's pre-oedipal phase in understanding female sexuality can be now translated as how does the little girl negotiate her castration complex in the pre-Oedipal stage?

Moreover, consider the following. The negotiation of the Oedipus complex is central in the construction of subjectivity, personality, attributes, and sexuality, and all of these organisations begin to take place because the child faces the threat of castration. That is if, according to Freudian theory, the child in question is a boy. Now we can begin to question whether, in the case of the little girl, these central organisations that are at the core of one's existence happen in a similar fashion, since the threat of castration does not exist. Does the little girl enter the Oedipus complex at all? If she *does* enter, what destroys her Oedipus complex? Does she ever give up her oedipal position? What motivates her to do so? Furthermore, if, in Freudian terms, the Oedipus complex lays the foundation of the superego, how can we conceptualise the construction of the little girl's superego, since she might not have ever entered or come out of her oedipal position? Does that mean that the castration complex for the little girl continues to operate even past her childhood? These are essential questions that one needs to consider when reading Freudian texts, particularly "Female sexuality" (1931b).

At the same time, it is important to momentarily hold back our urge to operate from a position of social equality when it comes to psychoanalytic theories and Freud's conceptualisation of female sexuality. Yes, Freudian theories of sexuality do not perceive the little girl's psychosexual development as similar to that of the little boy, but it is not matter of equality or rights, it is a matter of the psychical consequences of the anatomical differences. It is, rather, a matter of the differences in psychical negotiation of realities and their effects in our adult lives. However, in the same breath, it can also be argued that Freud's formulation of the castration complex does not perceive the little girl in any way different than the little boy in their pre-oedipal phase. The following theoretical formulations indicate this symmetry.

1. Although their experiences vary widely and the psychical consequences are different, both the little boy and the little girl *do* experience the castration complex in their early years.
2. Irrespective of the fact that girls anatomically do not possess a penis, in Freudian terms, at the phallic stage, both the little boy and the little girl know of only one genital, the male one.
3. Both the sexes have the same love-object at the beginning of their lives, the mother.

For the reasons listed above, I argue that it is a question of how the little girl's attachment with her first love object is affected (or not) by her experience of the castration complex. Sexuality is the key to unlocking the mystery behind all psychoneuroses, according to Freud. Within the context of the modern clinic and discourse on sexuality, understanding this pre-oedipal phase and the little girl's attachment to the mother that *belongs to this phase* are crucial because they are "intimately related to the aetiology of hysteria" (Freud, 1931b, p. 227). This statement is again confirmed when one reflects on Freud's earlier statement, made in relation to the Dora case history, ". . . it is the sexual function that I look upon as the foundation of hysteria and of the psychoneuroses in general" (1905e, p. 113). Examining human sexuality through the Freudian prism in this manner reveals that sexuality is, indeed, much more than one's orientation. Furthermore, Freud suggested that the connection between the little girl's pre-oedipal phase and the aetiology of hysteria becomes clearer "when we reflect that both the phase and the neurosis are characteristically feminine, and further, that in this dependency on the mother we have the germ of later paranoia in women" (1931b, p. 227). This statement is condensed and requires closer examination in parts.

In the statement quoted above, Freud referred to the pre-oedipal phase as "feminine" because of the passivity on the child's part and his or her dependency on the mother or the primary carer for existence during the first few years of life. To understand why "the neurosis" (hysteria) is being referred to by Freud as "characteristically feminine" one needs to turn to the symptoms presented in the clinic. First, "feminine" does not restrict itself to females; it is an attribute that can be embodied by a person of either gender. Second, patients often describe the symptoms of hysteria as certain things that are occurring and being done *to them*. The passivity in the patient's experience of the symptoms are strikingly similar to the passivity of the child's dependence on the mother during the early years of life. However, this "dependency", that is, the passivity of the girl's preoedipal phase, and Freud's choice of the phrase "characteristically feminine" are not to be mistaken for confirmation of the presence of a female libido in the little girl's pre-oedipal phase. Freud has repeatedly warned against such assumption. He clearly outlined the same in a letter to Dr Carl Muller-Braunschweig, whose work Freud equated with that of Horney, Jones, and other analysts who took up the biological stance in the great Freud–Jones debate and opposed Freud's phallic interpretation of femininity. Freud wrote, "We deal only with one libido which behaves in a male way" (Freud, 1971[1935], p. 329).

The remaining part of the statement quoted earlier, where Freud suggested that "in this dependency on the mother we have the germ of later paranoia in women" can be interpreted as the following. First, this is a statement that partly refers to clinical experiences that Freud encountered in his own work on hysteria and also from the reports of other analysts. Particularly, Ruth Mack Brunswick's work "The analysis of a case of paranoia" (Brunswick, 1929) is of great interest here, as the case clearly demonstrates how adult paranoia and delusional jealousy can be traced back to the patient's attachments belonging to the pre-oedipal stage, and that infantile sexuality plays a major part in the formation of the later symptoms. In this particular statement, then, Freud highlighted the connection between adult paranoia about being killed and its origination in the pre-oedipal phase of the fear of being devoured by the mother (1931b, p. 227). Considering that the child might develop hostility towards the mother as a consequence of the restrictions that the mother imposes on the child which are in line with the usual demands of hygiene, social norms, and the demands of civilisation in general, Freud inferred the following, "the mechanism of projection is favoured by the early age of the child's psychical organization" (1931b, p. 227), neaning that the hostility experienced by the little girl towards her mother due to the imposed restrictions is not processed by the infantile psyche for what it is and could express itself as the fear of being devoured by the mother, or even as the fear of being killed later on as an adult. The element of hostility is a major point of importance because not only does it play a crucial part in the girl's turning away from the mother, but also a number of other adult psychopathologies, such as masochism and sexual frigidity, can be traced back to this element.

As we shall see shortly, Freud returns to this topic in a more elaborated fashion in this text itself, which is discussed later below. For now, it is worth noting that Feud's disagreement with Lampl-de Groot's theory of the girl's negative Oedipus situation at the pre-oedipal stage (quoted above) was based precisely on the factor of hostility. Freud wrote that the exact point on which he found Lampl-de Groot's theory "inadequate is that it represents the turning-away from the mother as being merely a change of object and does not discuss the fact that it is accompanied by the plainest manifestations of hostility" (1931b, p. 241). Similarly, Freud also stated that it was Helena Deutsch, the Polish–American psychoanalyst, who did justice to the notion of hostility involved in the girl's turning away (Freud, 1931b, p. 241). For Deutsch, "feminine masochism is parallel to the masculine aggression" (Deutsch 1944, p. 191. In brief, this means, for Deutsch, the hostility involved in the girl's turning away from her mother can be interpreted as a transformation of her masculine aggressiveness into feminine masochism. If masculine aggressiveness is an activity directed outwards, then feminine masochism, for Deutsch, is to be understood as an activity directed inwards (Deutsch, 1944, p. 191). However, Freud disagreed with Deutsch on the point that she interpreted the little girl's pre-oedipal phallic activity as arising from identification with her father (Freud, 1931b, p. 242).

As mentioned above, the presence of "bisexuality" in the infantile stage is an extremely problematic factor that interferes with grasping a clear understanding of one's early object-choices and identifications. Within Freudian texts, bisexual disposition is an extremely complex subject. There is a detailed discussion of the concept of bisexuality in relation to female sexuality in Chapter Four. For now, it is important to highlight that the notion of bisexuality in women and its relation to the little girl's phallic stage were the prime topics in the Freud–Jones debate. Both of these notions were strongly objected to by Freud's opponents. As discussed before, the phallic stage is a developmental stage in Freud's writings, where, irrespective of their gender, both boys and girls know of only one genital organ—the male organ. Freud proposed earlier, in the 1920s, that the little girl in the phallic stage feels she has been castrated after her first accidental sight of the male organ. She might feel punished, inadequate, and jealous, could hope that it might grow one day, or she might also completely disavow the absence of the penis in herself (Freud, 1925j, pp. 251–253). In this 1931 text, Freud returns to both of these debated topics of bisexuality and the phallic stage of women. He clarifies that there is no question of denying the existence of the innate bisexual disposition in human beings and, moreover, the presence of the same is much clearer in women than in men (1931b, p. 228). He explained that this might be the case due to women having two leading sexual zones, the clitoris and the vagina, whereas men only have one, the penis. Based on clinical experiences and observations, Freud noted that with some exceptions, in the majority of cases for almost up until puberty, vaginal excitations remain virtually non-existent in girls and, similar to the penis for boys, the clitoris remains the chief genital organ for girls. This would mean that female sexual life is divided into two phases, where the first has masculine characteristics and the second feminine. Female sexual development, thus, requires a transition from the first phase to the second and this is something that is anything but parallel to the theories of male sexual development. According to Freud, this is one of the two tasks that the little girl must perform for the development of her femininity: abandonment of clitoral enjoyment and favouring the vagina as the chief genital zone.

For Freud, in addition to "the change in her own sex there must correspond a change in the sex of her object" (Freud, 1931b, p. 228). In other words, the little girl must also exchange her mother for her father as her new love object for the development of her femininity. Consider the case of the boy for whom his mother remains the love object until she is replaced by another, who possibly resembles her and fulfils the primary functions that are similar to those of his mother, such as caring, nourishing, and giving recognition. For the little boy, then, the psychosexual development is comparatively straightforward (at least, in the light of this current text) compared to the little girl's. Thus, it can be argued that psychopathologies in women can be traced back to how this transition took place, "how radically or how incompletely" it was carried out, and what are the "different possibilities" that presented themselves "in the course of this development" (1931b, p. 228). Hence, within the context of the modern clinic, it can be added that psychoanalytic listening goes beyond the usual periphery of popular psychological views, as it examines beyond the usual mechanisms of identification and projection. Such a technique of investigation and listening would require the practitioner to park their own anxiety, biases, and world views so that mainly three kinds of materials surface in the analysis:

- materials that have previously escaped conscious symbolisation;
- materials which indicate something about the patient's feminine sexual development;
- materials that have intimate connection to the patient's pre-oedipal phase.

Furthermore, Freud's choice of words, "change in her own sex", in the above comment emphasises and validates the very arguments of this book

For Freud, and in psychoanalysis, "sex" is neither just a biological organ nor the person's orientation, nor just an act of genital copulation. Rather, it is a position which can refer to a combination of all of that, but its origin lies in the workings of the person's mental life.

This position is neither a given, nor predetermined and, hence, Freud wrote "change in [her own] sex".

Returning to the text, we see that Freud further highlighted another striking difference between the sexes in relation to the Oedipus complex. In this regard, he suggested that it would be misleading to assume the analogy of "the Electra complex", as Jung used the term, because it is evident so far from Freud's clinical observations and theoretical constructs that psychosexual development between boys and girls are anything but parallel (Freud, 1931b, p. 229). It is only the male child who feels love for one parent and hatred for the other. Faced with the threat of castration, which becomes real after his accidental first sight of the female genital, the little boy goes through his Oedipus complex. This leads him to internalise the paternal agency and it contributes towards the formation of his superego. The formation of this agency is necessary for an individual to become a part of the civilised human race. In other words, the little boy's narcissistic investment in his penis provides him with the much-needed curbing of his infantile sexuality. The castration complex brings the little boy's Oedipus complex to an end. However, there is no such relevance of the "threat of castration" in the case of the little girl, for reasons that are obvious. Hence, her formation of the superego is up for debate and her Oedipus complex is much more difficult and different than that of the little boy. How does Freud come to that conclusion? Freud reformulates his theory of the little girl's Oedipus complex in the following way.

The girl's acknowledgement of her being castrated comes with the recognition of herself as inferior and males as superior, according to Freud (1931b, p. 229). In addition to this recognition, the little girl rebels against the injustice and Freud proposed that there are three possible "lines of development" that open up at this stage (p. 229). The first of these three leads to "general revulsion from sexuality" (p. 229). This is where the girl is dissatisfied with her apparent inferior equipment compared to that of the boys. She gives up on her "phallic activity" and her interest in sexuality in general disappears along with the best part of her masculinity (p. 229).

The second scenario is where she clings on to "her threatened masculinity" (p. 229). She continues to hope to gain a penis and to be a man until a much later stage of her life. According to Freud, such a "masculinity complex" might result, or manifest itself, in a girl's homosexual object choice (p. 230). It is only the third line of development that, if chosen, takes her to the "final normal female attitude", where she exchanges her mother for her father as her love object and finds herself in the "feminine form", or the positive form of the Oedipus complex (p. 230). This means, unlike men, for women the "Oedipus complex is the end-result of a fairly lengthy development" (p. 230).

Does this mean that women who did not choose the third line of development, did not exchange their first love object for the father, and did not exchange the clitoral enjoyment for the vaginal primacy are to be considered as not having entered the Oedipus complex? In those cases, theoretically, are we to understand that the castration complex did not influence the creation of, or did not lead them up to, the Oedipus complex? Compared to those who chose the third line of development, are these subjective positions to be considered as, perhaps, reacting differently to the limitation that the castration complex represents? Perhaps, in those cases, it can be argued that the intensity of their phallic activity overrides the horror of the discovery of castration.

While these are highly debatable questions, they are important to highlight because it makes one question the subjectivity of females, their chosen positions as a subject in relation to the Other, both in the Lacanian sense and the colloquial. Moreover, for Freud, while, for men, the castration complex brings the destruction of the Oedipus complex, for women, castration influences the creation of the Oedipus complex. In other words, Freud is alluding to the notion that, unlike men, women do not have to endure the "strongly hostile influences" of the castration complex (p. 230). This is why, for women, the "cultural consequences" for the destruction of the Oedipus complex and the urgency to do so are both very little (p. 230). Freud, thus, came to the conclusion that "it is this difference in the reciprocal relation between the Oedipus and the castration complex which gives its special stamp to the character of females as social beings" (p. 230).

It is evident, so far, that the pre-oedipal phase in women is of much more importance than in men because "many phenomena of female sexual life" that seemed unintelligible, Freud believes can be explained in reference to this phase (p. 230). For instance, incidences where women were believed to have chosen their partners "on the model of their father", or have placed them in a similar position and yet replicated with their husbands "their bad relations with their mother", can now seem intelligible in the light of this new-found theory (p. 231). In other words, a woman might have been influenced by her father's attributes and characteristics when choosing her husband. Yet, equally, there can also be a transference of her attitude towards her mother to her husband. Freud refers to this as the case of regression. This is because, in these cases, in the course of the relationship, the original attachment towards the mother which was repressed "emerges from repression" and the woman regresses from her attachment to her father back to this earlier state of attachment to her original love-object, the mother (p. 231).

Within the context of the wider society and the modern-day clinic, how are we to relate to these notions of regression? Clinical encounters would testify to these theories. In analysis, it is often discovered that patients would behave or speak in the same fashion regarding their male partners as they would about their mothers. No two subjects and their apparently same reactions are considered similar in psychoanalysis, precisely because of the subjective difference in all of us. However, it is not hard to recall instances where a female partner would accuse her male partner of not caring for her enough, not loving her enough, or not looking after the children better, as if he is not being a good mother to her child. These instances will be more relevant in the section below, where we discuss how Freud explained the reasons behind the little girl's turning away from her mother. For now, however, it must be added that, in analysis, when these moments are explored and further connections are made, it usually leaves the analysand shocked and surprised, precisely because these are unconscious connections which have never been brought to the analysand's conscious mind. In the light of this Freudian theory of the occurrence of coercion between a couple due to the woman's regression and the re-emergence of her original love object, a few questions arise.

Are we to consider that the mechanism of a similar regression does not take place in a man's life because he never turned away from his original love object? Yet, we can argue that he did. He replaced his original love object with something else that resembles her. However, since our society is predominately heterosexual in its orientation, it seems much more acceptable to have a man choosing a female partner who resembles his mother and behaving with her in a similar way as he did with his mother than a woman choosing a male partner who resembles her mother and behaving similarly to him as she did to her mother. Regardless, the knowledge of this theory of regression on the woman's part to her earlier object choice leading to the repetition of the earlier bad relation with her mother is potentially thought-provoking and useful, both within and outside the clinic.

At this stage, let us return to a bigger question. What factors influence the little girl's turning away from her mother "who was an object so intensely and exclusively loved" (p. 231)? Where and how can one find the element of hostility on which Freud placed so much importance? The first reason that Freud describes is jealousy of other people around the mother. The child demands exclusive possession and boundless love and attention. Hence, everyone around the mother is considered as a possible rival. Moreover, childhood love has "no aim and is incapable of obtaining complete satisfaction" (p. 231). This first love is, thus, destined to end in disappointment and this frustration gives rise to the "hostile attitude" (p. 231). However, similar to other romantic relations that do not achieve their aim, the "libidinal cathexis" remains uninterrupted and it continues. Stuck in an unsatisfying position, the libido then abandons the object and moves on to find a new one (p. 231). The second reason for her turning away from her mother is the effect of the castration complex, that is, her recognition of herself as inferior and without a penis. This opens three possible routes to her sexual development, as mentioned before: "(a) the one which leads to a cessation of her whole sexual life, (b) the one which leads to a defiant over-emphasis of her masculinity, and (c) the first steps towards definitive femininity" (1931b, p. 232). It would be misleading to consider these paths as clear-cut.

Moreover, Freud warns his reader that it would be rather a mistake to think that it is "easy to determine the exact timing" or even the "typical course of events" (p. 232). The point where the child makes his or her first discovery of castration varies, and it depends on numerous other factors that are not at all constant. These factors include everything about the child's surroundings, such as the number of siblings, their presence or absence, the time of their arrival, relations with playmates, the family dynamics, childcare arrangements, and so on. Furthermore, Freud suggests that various other factors also influence the child's chosen pathway to further psychosexual development, such as the girl's phallic activity, the level of its intensity, whether her activity was ever discovered or remained hidden, whether her enjoyment was ever interrupted or not, and so on (p. 232).

From a clinical perspective, it is important to note that the girl's own phallic activity influences her choice of sexual development route. This means a lot can be learnt about the patient's pre-oedipal phallic activity from the sexual development route she has chosen. But this is not a connection to be assumed; rather, this has to be discovered through analysis. Moreover, the girl's choice of path to sexual development is also influenced by whether or not her phallic activity was interfered with and "how much interference with it she experienced afterwards" (p. 232).

What is Freud referring to by the term "phallic activity"? Phallic activity refers to the little girl's discovery of clitoral excitement, which Freud described as "masturbation of the clitoris" (p. 232). Infantile masturbation for little girls only concerns the sensation of the clitoris and not the vagina (Freud, 1905d, p. 220). The sensation is usually discovered through accidental movement or as part of a game with older siblings or other children, or as part of the hygiene routine. Once discovered, children soon learn ways to recreate the sensations. Clinical observation suggested that nursery hygiene routines often provided material for the little girl to construct phantasies where the mother or the adult in charge played the part of the seducer. Actual seduction could also have occurred in some cases, intentionally or unintentionally on the adult's part and/or on an older sibling/playmate's part. However, seduction might intervene with the "natural course of the developmental processes, and it often leaves behind extensive and lasting consequences" (p. 232). This is perfectly understandable, as child abuse is undoubtedly a serious issue. However, psychoanalysis would go beyond the societal and ethical parameters. Psychoanalysis does not operate on the basis of ideologies; it operates based on the theories of drive. Hence, Freudian investigation would be exploring the child's reaction to abuse to understand how it was perceived by the subject and what imprint it left on the psyche. Freud suggests that once the child's new-found habit is discovered by an adult and prohibition of masturbation is established, the child finds a new motive for rebellion against the prohibitor. The ways the child rebels against the prohibitor are also equally important, as that, too, leaves a permanent mark in the psyche of the child. The infantile psychical organisation of the child often merges the mother with the mother substitutes in the phantasy as the prohibitor. Knowledge of the formation of these phantasies is key to uncovering the meanings of future psychopathologies. Importance should be placed on detaching ideologies so that an objective perspective of the patient's account is not disturbed. Allowing infantile sexual material such as this to surface requires skilful management of the clinician's own preconceived views and exploration of his own previous experiences. Engagement with psychoanalytic literature and taking up personal analysis are the two most efficient ways that such a position can be achieved.

So far, it is evident that the child's demand for the exclusive attention and boundless love from the mother, the girl's phallic activity, and the prohibition of masturbation are some of the key factors that influence the girl's turning away from her first love object, the mother. Now consider the second developmental route Freud outlined, "defiant over-emphasis of her masculinity" (p. 232). How does this developmental route influence the girl's turning away from the mother?

According to Freud, the girl's "defiant persistence in masturbation" opens up the path to masculinity and her object choice is influenced by this persistence (1931b, pp. 232–233). This is because clitoral enjoyment prevents the little girl from taking up the vagina as the chief genital zone. As mentioned above, this exchange of genital zone is one of the two essential tasks that she must complete to start her journey on the path leading to the development of her femininity. Freud observed that, in cases where the girl could not suppress her masturbation, analysis revealed that, even as an adult, she would make efforts to free herself from "a satisfaction which has been spoilt for her" (p. 232). Prohibition of masturbation is, thus, a crucial piece in the puzzle of the clinical picture. Resentment arising from the prohibition of sexual activity and enjoyment is a prime reason why the little girl detaches herself from her mother. This resentment is further strengthened when, during puberty, the child's mother "takes up her duty of guarding her daughter's chastity" (p. 233). This prohibition is also bestowed upon the little boy by the mother and, hence, the little boy, too, is provided with a "strong motive for rebellion" (p. 233).

Similarly, if the little girl chooses the path "towards definitive femininity" (p. 232), her discovery of her "own deficiency, from seeing a male genital" leaves her feeling wounded and she clings on to the idea of having the same equipment some day in the future (p. 233). Her hesitation and reluctance in accepting this anatomical difference leaves her with the wish to mend this injustice. Such a wish often "survives long after her hope has expired" (p. 233). Castration, which is, in this case, her discovery of the anatomical differences between the sexes, seems a misfortune not only to herself, but alao to the entire race of women. Such understanding taints her future concept of "femaleness" in general and of her mother (p. 233). The little girl might develop a perception of both these concepts as depreciating and lacking. Here, it must be noted that the impression of castration described by Freud and effects of prohibition of masturbation are theoretical constructs based on real observation and clinical practice. Materials such as these, when presented in a clinic during analysis, would strike one as "confusing and contradictory" (p. 233). Moreover, individual reactions to both castration and prohibition of sexual enjoyment would vary widely and "contrary attitudes" might exist side by side in the same person (p. 233). As Freud suggested, once prohibition is introduced, conflict begins to exist and this conflict "will accompany the development of sexual function" (p. 233). It is extremely difficult to distinguish and separate mental processes from the pre-oedipal phase to the later stages. This is because the later processes and experiences are overlaid on the previous ones and they often distort earlier memory. For example, memories in which she holds her father responsible for carrying out the punishment of castration for her "masturbatory activity" can be later construed by a female; however, neither of these ideas can be regarded as the primary one, according to Freud (p. 233). Because both the threat of castration and prohibition of masturbation usually come from the mother, at least the latter provides the girl with the motive to turn away from her first love object.

In addition to the girl's reproach against the mother for not providing her with a penis, she could also reproach her mother for not providing her with enough time at the breast, meaning that she might feel her mother did not suckle her enough, weaned her too early, or did not keep her at the breast for long enough (p. 234). Nourishment is necessary for survival and, hence, reproaches such as this have the potential to be distorted in the infantile psychical organisation and find later expression as a delusional belief in hatred, or fear of death, or as other complex symptoms. The "greed of a child's libido", her insatiable need and demand for exclusivity and, most importantly, the function of rapprochement towards the mother on her pathway to feminine sexual development, need to be considered while handling materials such as this. Moreover, it is useful to keep in mind that the formation of some of the motives for the little girl's turning away provided here are inevitable, due to the "nature of infantile sexuality", and others might appear to be rationalisation on the patient's behalf to make sense of the "uncomprehended change in feeling" (p. 234). Freud himself tried to make sense of this phenomenon in the following way, "perhaps the real fact is that the attachment to the mother is bound to perish, precisely because it was the first and was so intense" (p. 234).

At the same time, it would not be implausible to rule out the fact that the little girl also experiences an immense amount of affection towards her mother, along with the disappointments and reproach against her. It is absolutely possible to encounter cases where strong love coincides with equally strong hatred, and *vice versa*. In general, psychical organisations in the normal course of psychosexual development make it possible for an adult to separate love and hate just enough so that one does not feel compelled to hate their love-object or love the person they feel strong hatred against. Such coherence and organisation is the product of later developments (p. 235). Freud noted that the first phases of human sexual life are governed by ambivalence and many "retain this archaic trait all through their lives" (p. 235). It is especially evident in obsessional neurosis, where love and hate counterbalance each other in the patient's object-relationships (p. 235), which means that, in cases of obsessional neurosis, the same person or object is simultaneously loved or hated intensely by the subject, as was documented by Freud in the Rat-man case history (Freud, 1909d). Similarly, the little girl's attachment to her mother is ambivalent in nature and, coupled with other factors discussed above, she moves away from this primitive position. In some cases, adult psychopathologies are, thus, sophisticated versions of this more primitive intense attachment.

Aspects to reflect upon

At this point, it is necessary to pause and reflect on some of the characteristics of the pre-oedipal phase in the girl that Freud outlined. While it might seem from this text that the first two lines of development lead to paths where little girls have managed to somehow come to terms with their apparent feeling of loss (without penis) by either choosing to cease all of their sexual activity or by developing their masculine aspects, this is, however, not the case. These are not such clear-cut pathways and they are far from this apparent either/or paths to psychosexual development. However, in the light of this knowledge, a crucial aspect of the current societal discourse around us begs to be highlighted. When we speak of sexual frigidity, or a person's disinterest in sex, or even when we speak of a girl's apparent masculine trends, masculine personalities, we are often met with various colloquial terms. These are terms which sometimes highlight the difference in the person's outlook on life in comparison with that of the majority, her sexual orientation, her choice of activities, or even clothing at times. Sometimes, these terms are even used to define the person in her entirety. On many levels, the existence of these terms displays society's unwillingness to accept difference and its difficulties in perceiving beyond gender stereotype. One must also admit that these are very important and useful terms, as they "name" something that escapes symbolisation, something about the subject's sexuality. They name what cannot be named, they contain anxiety, and they provide a platform for identification. In other words, these terms provide the person with the much-needed thread to hold on to, helping her to establish a social bond and be integrated seamlessly in the fabric of larger society. This is, however, a social science perspective and not a psychoanalytic one.

Psychoanalysis enquires about the workings of the mental life of the speaking subject and, from a psychoanalytic perspective, the current social (including medical) atmosphere is at odds with the requisite space required for questions of subjectivity to emerge and be analysed. The problem lies where certain sets of behaviour, or outer makeup, of a person or his or her sexual orientation, are considered as a sign that corresponds to a certain category of human being. Moreover, a further problem lies where the categories in the social discourse become a person's identity, where one says, "I am that" and others validate "you are that". On the one hand, there is a current blurring between the medical discourse and one's own perception of oneself. For example, the *Diagnostic and Statistical Manual of Mental Disorders* (*DSM*) (American Psychiatric Association, 2013), through its discrete diagnostic terminologies, subtly provides the person with an identity by defining the person as not what *they have* or *are suffering from* but, rather, who *they are*: Mary is suffering from schizophrenia equals Mary *is* a schizophrenic.

On the other hand, there is a blurring between the social discourse and one's own perception. The current terms for one's sexual orientation are similarly discretely becoming one's identity: Jenny has never had any interest in sexual matters equals Jenny *is* asexual. Certain behavioural makeups are also currently corresponding in modern society with terms that describe one's sexual orientation. This is another blurring of one's behaviour and one's subjective sexual position. For example: Laura is a tomboy becomes Laura must be butch becomes Laura is a lesbian. It is particularly difficult and problematic, from a psychoanalytic perspective, if Mary, Jenny, and Laura are teenagers or young adults, or at an impressionable age in their lives and they begin to identify with these terms and become *that*.

In the light of the reading of this current text, one can argue that these ready-made identities and their wide availability in our society for a multitude of reasons are dampening subjective curiosity, which, if cultivated and nurtured, could form a question about one's subjective position. Formulation of such questions can lead to a much better understanding of one's own position as a subject, as an individual. Psychoanalysis and engagement with psychoanalytic literature such as this current text certainly embrace these questions and take them further, rather than stunting them and accepting the reality as it is without analysing its finer threads. At the same time, it is important to remember that clinical psychoanalytic work is aimed at helping those who *have* a question, which means, if a person is comfortable with the subjective position he occupies, psychoanalytic work does not intend to disturb the knitting of his existence. However, as psychoanalytically informed citizens of our society, we must question and analyse our own subjective positions each time we are contributing to the creation of a breathable space for those who are different. We must question whether our willingness to help is informed by ideological ethics; whether we are too quick to name, due to our own fear of the unknown and keenness to support and soothe those who do not fit in; whether our rushed approach to support those who are struggling with their being is actually helping them cope with their difficulties and flourish further or eliminating future possibilities of them exploring further.

Let us turn to the path described by Freud as "normal" development of femininity. Consider situations where the little girl becomes a woman and has a child of her own. We are all familiar with scenarios where the arrival of a new baby did not leave the mother with the contentment she expected. There are terms like "postnatal depression" and "baby blues" that attempt to describe such difficulties that the new mother experiences. Although *DSM-5* does not consider these terms as disorders, the suffering and the pain experienced does not become any less real. Depression, anxiety, phobia, and development of obsessive compulsion disorders are highly possible manifestations during the perinatal period. This period generally refers to the time from a woman's second trimester of pregnancy to the end of the second year after the birth. How can we relate this current discussion of the Freudian text in hand to someone suffering from perinatal psychiatric disorders?

Consider the following points: the little girl at her pre-oedipal stage demands exclusive attention and boundless love from her mother, but it ends in disappointment; the little girl's phallic activity or, rather, clitoral masturbation as Freud calls it, is prohibited by the mother, meaning the mother prevents her from deriving sexual enjoyment, which gives rise to hostility and frustration in the little girl; she also accuses her mother of not nourishing her enough; she feels her mother has wounded her quite literally, as she has brought her into the world with inferior equipment; her feelings towards her mother are also ambivalent. Now, if these points were translated in terms of the mother–child relation within a perinatal psychiatric clinic, then the complaints of the new mother would seem to be the following.

In the popular discourse related to pregnancy and motherhood there is a general expectation that the mother is to devote all her time, love, attention, and boundless affection to the new child, even though she might not feel the same. This other's demand is strikingly similar to that which the woman once demanded herself from her mother when she was a little girl. Moreover, the arrival of a child interferes with the parental couple's existing sexual relations and temporarily prevents the mother from continuing, or creating new, sexual relations. This can be perceived as a similar situation to the prohibition of masturbation and the interference with sexual enjoyment that she once experienced from her own mother. With regard to the reproach for inadequate nourishment provided by her mother, it is a similar worry that new mothers have for the baby, "Am I feeding the baby enough?" This is particularly distressing for patients who wish to breastfeed and yet do not produce enough milk, or have a baby whose hunger seems extraordinary to the mother. Furthermore, the feeling of inadequacy that the mother experiences when faced with the baby's unending and insatiable demands in these cases might also bring back the feeling of her being wounded (impression of castration).

Pregnancy changes a woman's body, both internally and externally. Some of these changes are permanent, such as scars from C-section, stretch marks on the tummy and thighs, changes in the breast, and, in cases of vaginal delivery the shape of the vagina itself might change permanently and, in some cases, it affects the woman's sexual life.

It is not unusual for a woman to experience the feeling of injustice, left with inferior equipment after birth, just as she did in the pre-oedipal phase when she first recognised the anatomical differences between the sexes. Moreover, ambivalence is a common theme in the perinatal clinic and it is not at all unusual to hear the patient experience intense hatred and love simultaneously towards her baby, just as she experienced ambivalence towards her mother during her pre-oedipal phase.

It is naturally distressing to hear anyone suffering in any form, but when it comes to hearing about a new mother struggling to slip into the role of the carer, the nurturer, there are several alarm bells that immediately go off. Practitioners are immediately on guard, ready to act, report the incident, and follow the usual protocol. Following protocols is crucial and essential, particularly because the relevant people here are vulnerable. It is not just a matter of the mother's mental health that is in question, but also her safety and, what is more, the baby's wellbeing is in question. Hence, it is completely understandable why practitioners would be highly anxious and eager to help when hearing about a new mother's distressing experiences regarding her baby. The knowledge of these resemblances have the potential to help the clinician contain her own anxiety faced with these complaints from her patients, and, equally, this piece of knowledge has the potential to help the patient make sense of her "uncomprehended change in feeling", to use Freud's words.

This view of the mother–child relationship, translated in light of the little girl's pre-oedipal experiences in this fashion, goes beyond the popular psychological theories of identification because it brings to light the intensity, obscurity, and the importance of the knowledge of infantile sexuality and how dominant it is in the human psyche.

Finally, in the light of these views, one can also pose a larger question, "what is the child for the mother?": an extension of her first love object; a trauma re-experienced? The emphasis should be placed on the fact that whether it is a set of behaviours, or a certain sexual orientation, or one of the most common events of human difficulty, such as a baby's arrival leading to changes in the family, psychoanalysis does not accept it as a given. Psychoanalysis questions "what is going on" rather than accepting it as "that is that".

* * *

The swing-over

Returning to the text in hand, Freud further explores the nature of the little girl's attachment to her mother during the pre-oedipal phase (what does she require of her mother, what are her demands) (1931b, p. 234). Similar to the girl's ambivalent attitude towards the mother, her sexual aim, too, is partially passive and partially active. Her sexual aim towards her mother is also determined by the libidinal phases as she passes through the oral, anal, and phallic stages. Freud placed importance on the child's "swing-over from passivity to activity" which does not occur "with the same regularity or vigour in all children" and in some children "it may not occur at all" (p. 236). What is this "swing-over" he is referring to? Drawing from clinical experience and his observation of children's play, Freud concluded that "in every field of mental experience", including the field of sexuality, when a child "receives a passive impression", he tries to "produce an active reaction" (p. 236). In an effort to master the external world, the child is inclined to do himself what has been done to him. Since, at the pre-oedipal stage, both the little girl and the little boy know of only one genital, that is, the penis, and since both have the same love-object, the mother, the use of the male pronoun "him" should not exclude the little girl here. For example, in children's play, the child can be seen playing doctor with a younger playmate and repeating what he himself has experienced helplessly in the doctor's clinic at some point. The same is true for the little girl. It can be also interpreted as the child's attempt at "supplementing a passive experience with an active piece of behaviour", in order to annul the previous one (p. 236). Freud considered it as a "revolt against passivity and a preference for the active role" (p. 236). The "swing-over" is, then, a reflection of the "relative strength of the masculinity and femininity" that the child will exhibit in his or her sexuality (p. 236).

The oldest sexually coloured experiences

In the light of the pre-oedipal phase, the first "sexually coloured experiences" that the child receives can be considered as passive as the child is "suckled, fed, cleaned, dressed . . . and taught to perform" all relevant functions (p. 236). While the child enjoys the passive position in these activities, a part of her libido also wants to turn them around. The child's spontaneous suckling at the breast and the gradual learning of independence can be regarded as her attempt to become self-sufficient or to take up a more active position. Using this chain of thought, Freud draws attention to the little girl's occasional request to swap places with her mother, "Now let's play that I'm the mother and you're the child" (p. 237). Such a request, as Freud argues, is undoubtedly a good example of the little girl's "swing-over from passivity to activity". However, the best example of the little girl's attempt at transitioning from passivity to activity is her play with her dolls, "where she represents the mother and the doll the child" (p. 237). This common sight of femininity is truly an expression of "the *active* side of femininity", according to Freud (p. 237). In addition, the little girl's exclusive attachment to her mother and her "complete neglect of her father-object" also find expression in this activity (p. 237). This perspective of femininity puts the view of the mother–child relationship into a different light. Moreover, in the light of Freud's observation, one has to rethink the commonly considered equivalency of the term "passivity" to the concept of "femininity" and "femaleness".

Freud acknowledges that it is impossible to obtain a detailed account of the girl's oral, sadistic, and phallic trends towards her mother because these are "obscure instinctual impulses" that the child is incapable of psychically grasping at the time of their occurrence (p. 237). However, from clinical experiences, Freud noted that they occur chronologically and, in analysis, they are usually presented as distorted, as if they were directed towards the father-object. For example, the little girl's active libidinal impulses towards her mother can be seen in her aggressive oral and sadistic wishes to devour the mother, or even as death-wish against her mother. Such wishes can be transformed by early repression and find later expression in the fear of being killed by the mother. Since it is the *mother* who provides nourishment, both for the boy and the girl, the *mother* is the first love-object and, given that the girl's position towards her *mother* is ambivalent, it would be a mistake to regard such a fear presented in the clinic as originating from the father-object. However, Freud suggests that it is plausible to think that, since the first love-relation with the mother is destined to end in disappointment and the possible next object-choice *is* the father, repression does an excellent job in distorting those first "sexual or sexually coloured experiences" (p. 236) of the child in relation to the mother. Moreover, when a child turns away from her mother, she "also makes over to her father her introduction into sexual life" (p. 238), which is why, often, the father-object appears in the phantasies of later years as the "sexual seducer" while the one who initiated this apparent seduction was the mother. The seduction in question is usually the child's interpretation of memories of the "strongest, genital sensation when they were being cleaned" or, possibly, being toilet trained by their mother (p. 238).

The phallic phase is accompanied by the girl's active instinctual wishes directed towards her mother, and clitoral masturbation is the prime sexual activity during this time (1931b, p. 239). Freud clarified, here, that the idea of the mother accompanying this activity is a probability. He added, "whether the child attaches a sexual aim to the idea, and what that aim is, I have not been able to discover from my observation" (p. 239). However, the aim becomes recognisable around the time of the arrival of a new sibling. Similar to the boy, the little girl's reaction to this arrival is a complete ignorance of the father's role in the matter. She believes that she herself has gifted the baby to her mother (p. 239). Such a reaction has been previously documented in Freud's earlier case history of "Little Hans" (1909b). Hans, the five-year old boy, reshaped his family tree in his phantasy, especially after the birth of his little sister, Hanna. Obscurity is the prime characteristic of infantile sexuality. Hence, the construction of phantasy that is at work in the tender psychical organisation of a child and the imprints it leaves behind are bound to baffle everyone. This is why Freud wrote, "no doubt this sounds quite absurd, but perhaps that is only because it sounds so unfamiliar" (1931b, p. 239).

It is evident from the reading so far that the girl's turning away from her mother in her pre-oedipal stage is not just a "mere change of object" (p. 239). It is an extremely crucial and complex step towards the development of her femininity. The "lowering of her active impulses" and the "rise of the passive ones" toward her mother is a parallel process to her turning away from the mother (p. 239). It is the increased passive aims that turn the little girl away from her clitoral masturbatory habits, helps her repress her early masculinity, and assists her in her transition to choosing her father as the love-object. However, this process is not the same for every little girl. Moreover, the effects and expressions of the "remains of the pre-Oedipal attachment to her mother" varies widely (p. 239). The point to note here is the similarities of the "libidinal forces at work", both in the boy and the girl, at the early stage. Both have the same love-object, the mother, and both have active wishful impulses towards their mother. In the case of the girl, the difference in anatomy, the "biological factors", as Freud puts it, help to deflect her active libidinal forces and direct "masculine trends into feminine channels" (p. 240). The term "biological factor" is to be understood as the existence of the vagina in the girl and, hence, the sensation attached to this organ soon makes itself felt.

*   *   *

Chemical excitation or . . .?

It must be acknowledged, at this stage, that the terms "feminine", "masculine", "active", and "passive" have social constructions attached to them and their definitions will vary across disciplines such as social science and pure science, to name but a couple. Matters become rather complicated when these terms are questioned from the perspective of bio-chemistry, a discipline that is comparatively known to be more certain of its findings. For example, male liver, muscles, brain cells, and fat cells produce oestrogen, which is usually known to be a female reproductive hormone, while various locations in the female body, such as the ovaries, adrenal gland, and the peripheral tissues, to name but few, produce testosterone, usually referred to as the male sex hormone. This means that both of these hormones co-exist in both males and females, but in different levels. Can hormones be a reliable marker for masculinity and femininity? At a strictly biological level, the answer is positive, but only to a certain extent. While physical changes and the determination of one's sex are influenced by hormones, sexual excitation, however, does not necessarily depend on bio-chemistry.

For example, consider testosterone. It is known as the sex hormone for men, because it works towards the growth of the man's secondary sex characteristics. It also stimulates the sex drive for men, but it is *not* the only factor that causes sexual excitation in men. In fact, a low level of testosterone rarely leads to erectile dysfunction and does not always result in low sex drive in a man. So, it is not solely testosterone that is responsible for male sexual excitation. Now, consider,

oestrogen, which causes the development of secondary sexual characteristic in females. It regulates the functioning of the menstrual cycle
and it is an important reproductive hormone. However, it cannot be
considered as solely responsible for causing sexual excitation in
females. In fact, the idea of testosterone as a possible cure for female
sexual dysfunction has generated an almost equal amount of inconclusive studies as studies that have looked at oestrogen as a possible
cure for the same.

Male sexual dysfunction, particularly erectile dysfunction, is an
extremely complex disorder and has several dimensions and aetiologies attached to it. Sometimes, physicians might prescribe Viagra to
treat erectile dysfunction. It is a prescription drug that is usually known
to help the patient obtain and sustain an erection, mainly by causing
increased blood flow. Erection, however, should not necessarily be
equated with the presence of sexual urges in a man. Interestingly,
for women's sexual dysfunctions, which are also multi-dimensional,
complex, and have various aetiologies attached to them, the popular
medical treatments include hormone therapy, and a new FDA
approved, state of the art medication called Flibanserin, a non-hormone
prescription pill. As mentioned above, hormone therapy is yet to
show conclusive result across the board and Flibanserin, too, has a
very low response rate. Does that mean that, from a bio-chemistry perspective, what sexually excites a woman still remains a mystery?

These observations will seem more intriguing in relation to Freud's
comment from the current text, dated 1931, where he hoped that some
day biochemistry will "disclose a substance to us whose presence
produces a male sexual excitation and another substance which
produces a female one" (1931b, p. 240). Hence, if one asks whether
there have been any such two distinct substances identified for males
and females almost a century later, the answer will be disappointing.
If such a distinction between feminine and masculine sexual excitation, from a bio-chemistry perspective, seems blurry and it does not
provide much insight into feminine sexuality, then it seems plausible
to consider the following two propositions.

1. The mechanisms of complex psychical processes that influence a
    man or a woman's sexuality would have to rely on a different
    marker.
2. That the knowledge of feminine sexuality will mostly remain
    outside the grasp of empirical science.

Freud dedicated a lifetime of research into examining terms such as feminine, masculine, active, and passive. In brief, from a social science perspective, Freud agrees that every individual displays mixture of character traits belonging to both sexes and everyone exhibits a combination of activity and passivity which might not tally with their biological sex (1905d, pp. 219–220), which means that he agreed that "pure masculinity and femininity remain theoretical constructions of uncertain contents" (1925j, p. 258). Freud has also urged his readers not to describe the two opposite currents that run through human sexual life as "masculine" and "feminine". Rather, he suggested that it is more beneficial to refer to them as "active" and "passive" (1905d, p. 198). "Sexual chemistry", as Freud called it, still finds it difficult to isolate distinct substances responsible for sexual excitation and the search for "different exciting factors of hysteria, obsessional neurosis, melancholia" too (1931b, p. 240) still remains inconclusive in 2017, just as it was in 1931. Freud proposes that using the marker of "active" and "passive" is much more beneficial precisely because psychoanalysis is not concerned with "whether there is a single sexually exciting substance in the body or two or countless numbers of them" (1931b, p. 240). Rather, it is concerned with the management of a single libido, which has "both active and passive aims" (p. 240). By aims, Freud is referring to the "modes of satisfaction" (p. 240). Furthermore, libido is never without an aim. This is because the drive always seeks something; in other words, the drive is always active. Hence, even with a passive aim, the libido is masculine, "we deal only with one libido which behaves in a male way" (Freud, 1971[1935], p. 329).

To sum up, this chapter has provided a close reading of the Freudian text titled "Female sexuality" (1931b) with the aim of highlighting the connection between the negotiation of the castration complex and human psychosexual development. This was achieved by examining the theoretical contents and presenting them in a simpler language for a wider audience. Since the aim was to shed light on understanding how one becomes a male or a female and with regard to the Freudian concept of castration, this chapter has raised few questions that have opened space for future discussion. The relevance of the pre-oedipal stage in a girl and its relation to further psychopathologies are evident from this discussion. It has also been highlighted how, for Freud, there is only one libido and that is active, even though it has passive aims.

For Freud, the little girl acts in a similar fashion to the little boy in her pre-oedipal phase and directs her active libidinal wishes, like the little boy, towards her love-object, the mother. The various factors that influence her to turn away from the mother have also been highlighted. It is evident that the little girl's phallic activity, her clitoral enjoyment, the patterns of interruptions in her enjoyment, together with the possible path she chooses from the moment she discovered anatomical differences between the sexes and, most of all, the imprints that all of these leave behind in her psyche, all contribute towards her psychosexual development. Moreover, the chapter has illustrated that what truly sexually excites a woman still remains a mystery, even from the perspective of endocrinology and biochemistry. The complexity and difficulty involved in defining female psychosexual development have been highlighted throughout. Freud's examination of the process of how a little girl becomes a woman only illustrates the very point that feminine sexuality is a riddle, psychical mechanisms are complex, and defining obscure instinctual impulses would seem not yet possible, in spite of the best efforts made.

Before moving on to a similarly structured close reading of the second Freudian text in question, "Femininity" (1933a), where Freud has further explored the element of bisexuality present in a woman, it is essential to examine Freud's position with regard to the theory of bisexuality.

CHAPTER FOUR

A brief introduction to bisexual disposition and its place within Freud's psychoanalytic theories

Introduction

This chapter provides a brief introduction to the theory of bisexuality and its place within psychoanalytic theories. It is an extremely complex topic and yet highly relevant and essential in order to understand how female sexuality and femininity are theorised in psychoanalytic literature. The aim of this chapter is to introduce few important and essential elements of psychoanalytic theories that will be used later to illustrate how psychoanalytic understanding of femininity is very different than that of the social and human sciences. This is done by first outlining how the theory of bisexuality drew Freud's attention. Next, I describe Freud's position in relation to the theory of bisexuality and how he situates this theory in relation to his own theories of psychoanalysis.

Freud's introduction to bisexuality

The idea of bisexuality was introduced to Freud by the German physician and close acquaintance of Freud, Wilhelm Fleiss (1858–1928). For

Fleiss, bisexuality was a universal attribute of all human beings. He also considered that bisexuality is a physiological fact that has a considerable impact on the formation and development of human psychoneuroses. However, Fleiss's theory of bisexuality relied heavily on biology. Freud was sceptical of theories that would extend biological hypotheses to the sphere of the psyche. Based on anatomical and embryological findings, Freud agrees that a certain amount of anatomical hermaphroditism is present in every individual, meaning that traces of the apparatus of the opposite sex are found in an atrophied state in both male and female anatomy in cases of normal development. Certain secondary sexual characteristics of the opposite sex are also often found in normal development. Secondary sexual characteristics are physical developments that occur during puberty; they are used as markers for distinguishing between the sexes and they are not directly involved in reproduction. In abnormal and extremely rare cases, it is difficult to determine the sex of the person in whom true hermaphroditism has occurred. In cases where both sets of organs are found, frequently both are in an atrophied condition. In normal development, it can be supposed that "an original bisexual physical disposition has, in the course of evolution, become modified into a unisexual one, leaving behind only a few traces of sex that has become atrophied" (Freud, 1905d, p. 141). For Fliess, this "course of evolution" was similar to the psychical mechanism that Freud described as repression. In other words, Fliess broadened an anatomical theory to the theory of the mind.

In "'A child is being beaten'" (1919e), Freud evaluated Fliess's theory and noted that, according to Fliess, "the motive force of repression in each individual is a struggle between the two sexual characters" (Freud, 1919e, p. 200). This means that the dominant sex of a person, having won the battle of the initial struggle for the determination of sex at an anatomical level, eventually represses "the mental representation of the subordinated sex into the unconscious" (1919e, p. 200). Thus, according to Fliess, the nucleus of the unconscious, which is, in terms of the Freudian theory of repression, denoted as "the repressed", carries the characteristics of the opposite sex (1919e, p. 201). To put it simply, according to Fliess's theory, in the case of men, their "unconscious and repressed can be brought down to feminine instinctual impulses" and *vice versa* for women (1919e, p. 201) (instinctual impulses are explained further below). In this same text,

Freud indicated that he considered this theory to be both "incorrect and misleading" (Freud, 1919e, p. 200).

Freud's position

Freud, although he never clarified his position in relation to the theory of bisexuality, did, however, on various occasions, outline his difficulties in accepting the positions of theorists who extend anatomical hypotheses to the psychical sphere. One such occasion resulted in the article "'A child is being beaten'" (1919e, p. 200), as discussed above. Towards the beginning of the twentieth century, various theorists were linking non-heterosexuality to physical disposition. Fliess was not the only theorist who placed high biological importance on the theory of bisexuality. For example, Havelock Ellis, an English physician whose research interest was human sexuality, accorded utmost importance to "the secondary and tertiary sexual characters and to the great frequency of the occurrence of those of the opposite sex in inverts" (Freud, 1905d, p. 142). Freud acknowledged the frequency of these occurrences and considered them as "indications of hermaphroditism", but did not believe that the presence of secondary or tertiary sexual characters belonging to the opposite sex necessarily influences the subject's "change of sexual object in the direction of inversion" (Freud, 1905d, p. 142).

According to Freud, Austro-German psychiatrist Richard Krafft-Ebing is another theorist of human sexuality whose views on bisexuality could be seen as "replacing the psychological problem by the anatomical one" (Freud, 1905d, p. 142). According to Krafft-Ebing, bisexual disposition provides every individual with "masculine and feminine brain centres as well as with somatic organs of sex", only, at puberty, these "centres" develop under the influence of the "sexgland" and, at the beginning of life, the sex gland is independent of these "centres" (1905d, p. 143). One of the major reasons for Freud's rejection of this view was the uncertainty of the existence of such centres in the human brain, set aside purely for sexual functions (1905d. p. 143).

Freud further rejected the views of several other theorists of his time in relation to the notion of bisexuality, such as those who considered bisexuality as an explanation *of* inversion and those who derived the theory of bisexuality *from* inversion (1905d, p. 143). According to Freud, hypothetical psychical hermaphroditism and anatomical hermaphroditism has no close connection (1905d, p. 142). In other words, for Freud, "inversion[s]" (1905d, p. 136), which can be translated as homosexuality and "somatic hermaphroditism", are completely independent of each other (1905d, p. 136). Austrian physician Hans von Halban also supported this view, according to Freud, and this is evident in Freud's comment, "occurrences of individual atrophied organs and of secondary sexual characters are to a considerable extent independent of one another" (1905d, p. 142).

In response to Fliess's theory, Freud draws from his clinical observation and criticised Fleiss's proposition on the following grounds. In "Analysis terminable and interminable" (1937c), Freud explains that Fliess's theory sexualises the psychical process of repression (1937c, p. 251), meaning that Fliess's proposition explains the theory of bisexuality on "biological grounds instead of on purely psychological ones". One of the reasons behind Freud's position is outlined in "'A child is being beaten'" (1919e). In this text, Freud drew from his clinical observation and concluded that "both in male and female individuals masculine as well as feminine instinctual impulses are found, and that each can equally well undergo repression and so become unconscious" (Freud, 1919e, p. 202). Such findings contradict Fleiss's theory because it suggested that the subject's manifest sexual characteristics would always be only on the side of the repressing force and the sexual characteristics belonging to the opposite sex would always remain on the side of the repressed (Laplanche & Pontalis, 1973, p. 53). The universality of this statement is, thus, questionable and it clearly contradicted the findings of Freud's clinical observation. Hence, Freud warned his readers against sexualising the "motive forces of repression" (1919e, p. 203).

In the following comment from "Analysis terminable and interminable", Freud seemed also to agree with Fleiss's view, as he noted that, in analysis, he often encountered instances where "the attitude proper to the opposite sex . . . has succumbed to repression" (1937c, p. 251). The observations that led Freud to make this comment, the context within which it was made, and what Freud intended by it require closer inspection. This is done in Chapter Five, when we examine the Freudian text "Femininity" (Lecture XXXIII, 1933a). For now, however, it is important to note two points.

1.   The resistance, or "biological bedrock", that Freud refers to in "Analysis terminable and interminable" (1937c, p. 252) is in relation to the castration complex and it is not based on biological grounds, such as Fleiss's theory of bisexuality suggests.

2.   In the same paper, Freud credited Fliess with bringing his attention to this particular aspect, but he also continued to disagree with Fliess's view in the following fashion. He wrote,

> Fliess was inclined to regard the antithesis between the sexes as the true cause and primal motive force for repression. I am only repeating what I said then in disagreeing with his view, when I decline to sexualize repression in this way – that is, to explain it on biological grounds instead of on purely psychological ones. (Freud, 1937c, p. 251)

"Antithesis between the sexes"

Bisexual disposition, thus, according to Freud, is independent of the subject's physical characteristics. Apart from the above reasons, Freud also had other reservations and doubts about the theory of bisexuality. For instance, the concept of bisexual disposition itself presupposes "a clear grasp of antithesis between masculinity and femininity" (Laplanche & Pontalis, 1973, p. 53), but what do these terms mean? Freud pointed out at several stages of his life that the meaning of the terms "masculine" and "feminine" vary widely within different contexts and schools, hence "a clear grasp" of these terms is rather problematic. While these terms might seem unambiguous to a lay person, they are extremely confusing among various schools of science. In 1915, Freud outlined the three most common uses of these terms and added them to his *Three Essays on the Theory of Sexuality* in a footnote (Freud, 1905d, p. 219).

"Masculine" and "feminine" are terms that are often used to denote activity and passivity, in a biological sense and in a sociological sense.

It is the first use of these terms that Freud regarded as the most relevant in psychoanalysis and he considered that although the theory of bisexuality as described by Fleiss is important and useful, it cannot easily be connected to the cornerstone of psychoanalysis, which is the theory of instincts (drive, or *Trieb*). The immediate questions at this stage are: why did Freud prefer to refer to masculine and feminine as active and passive rather than the other two uses of the terms, what is the theory of instincts, and why did Freud think that the theory of bisexuality is difficult to connect to the theory of instincts? These questions are attended to in the following sections, in the order shown above.

Why the preference for activity and passivity over the other two uses of the terms?

Let us begin with *why not* the second and the third usage of these terms? The second use of these terms that Freud referred to is the field of biology. The biological definition is the easiest application of these terms, where "'masculine' and 'feminine' are characterized by the presence of spermatozoa or ova respectively and by the functions proceeding from them" (Freud, 1905d, p. 219). Biological masculinity is usually linked with activity, "powerful muscular development, aggressiveness, greater intensity of libido"; however, there are many instances where the female of the species has these qualities (Freud, 1905d, p. 220). Freud returned to this point again in *Civilization and Its Discontents* (1930a) and noted that biology often uses activity and passivity as markers to identify the difference between the sexes where, more often, maleness is identified with activity and femaleness with passivity. Freud did not consider it a reliable marker, as the animal kingdom often proves this universal claim untenable (1930a, p. 106).

The third use of these terms that Freud referred to is from the field of sociology. Here, the meaning of these terms is derived from the observation of actual individuals who display these qualities. Sociological observation frequently confirms that, in both a psychological sense and a biological sense, pure masculinity or femininity cannot be found in human beings. Freud, thus, reminded his readers that every individual "displays a mixture of the character-traits belonging to his own and to the opposite sex", and a "combination of activity and passivity" is also found in every human being's character traits even though, at times, they do not "tally with the biological" sex of the person (Freud, 1905d, p. 220). With relation to bisexual disposition, it is necessary at this point to outline Freud's remark on the terms "masculine" and "feminine", again from *Civilization and Its Discontents* (1930a), which is, in fact, one of the major textbooks in both sociology and social psychology. Here, Freud considered that "man is an animal organism with (like others) an unmistakably bisexual disposition" (1930a, p. 105). Consider that human beings are an integration of "two symmetrical halves" (1930a, p. 105). While some theorists claim that each half is purely male and female, Freud argued that these halfs could also have been "originally hermaphrodites" (1930a, p. 105). A further problem arises when "sex", which is a biological fact that affects mental life, is to be comprehended psychologically. This is mainly because, using anatomy, "characteristics of maleness and femaleness" can be pointed out, but psychology cannot do the same. This view not only supports Freud's earlier arguments that biological sex has no correlation with the person's characteristics (femaleness and maleness), but it also points to an important aspect of human sexuality—that a portion of the person's sex will always remain out of the grasp of the discipline of psychology. Hence, the sociological meaning of the terms is also not reliable. How does one learn more about this aspect of "sex"-uality that remains out of the grasp of psychology? What markers are to be used in that case?

Freud proposed that it is the theory of the instinct that is useful for understanding human sexuality and that the psychoanalytic meaning of activity and passivity is a far more reliable marker in learning about human sexuality than others. In 1924, Freud added a footnote to the *Three Essays on the Theory of Sexuality* and noted that the theory of instinct "is the most important but at the same time the least complete portion of psychoanalytic theory" (1905d, p. 168). Details of this theory, hence, are outside the scope of this book. However, for now, this will be explained briefly in relation to the current discussion on bisexual disposition and the major question on sexuality, using material from *Three Essays on the Theory of Sexuality* (1905d). One of the reasons for focusing on this text is that it is in the *Three Essays* that bisexuality is discussed by Freud in more detail than elsewhere (1905d, pp. 141–144). In order to understand what the theory of instincts is and why Freud thought that the theory of bisexuality has very little connection to it, it is important to highlight how the topic of bisexuality came about in his investigation into human sexuality.

What led the discussion on bisexuality in Three Essays*?*

The topic of bisexuality came as part of the discussion on "inverts"; as mentioned above, it was a term used in the popular discourse around Freud's time to describe those who had "contrary sexual feelings", and it was also part of a bigger discussion, "sexual aberrations" with which Freud began his *Three Essays on the Theory of Sexuality* (1905d, p. 136). One of the major reasons for beginning his essays with the subject of sexual aberrations was that, from both his clinical and general observations, Freud began to notice that human sexuality in general is obscure and, hence, "contrary sexual feelings" are not just restricted to those who are labelled as inverts, perverts, or others who are considered to be going beyond the social norms. Drawing from his observations of both children and adults, Freud was about to formulate his theories on human sexuality. As he explored "inversion", he reviewed the literature that conceptualised bisexuality as one of the explanations of inversion. The discussion on inversion in the light of bisexuality opened up further questions and the uncertainty of formulating a general theory on sexual aberrations was becoming apparent.

This led Freud to conclude that his investigation, although it did not provide a solution to the puzzle of sexual aberrations, it did, however, bring forward a very important "piece of knowledge" (1905d, p. 146). He noted that ". . . we have been in the habit of regarding the connection between the sexual instinct and the sexual object as more intimate than it in fact is" (1905d, p. 148). This observation is confirmed by his experience of working on cases which are "considered abnormal", where it is evident that "the sexual instinct and the sexual object are merely soldered together" (1905d, p. 148): for example, cases of fetishism and perversion in the social sense (the psychoanalytic sense of these terms is different and is explained in Chapter Seven). In "normal" cases, this is not so noticeable because the object seems "part and parcel of the instinct" (1905d, p. 148). Thus, he questioned the very essence of normality and believed that his discussion would encourage his readers to question the same by loosening "the bond that exists in our thoughts between instinct and object" (1905d, p. 148).

It can be argued that, in a way, for Freud, the discussion on sexual aberration and bisexuality finally led him to theorise human sexuality as the following, "it seems probable that the sexual instinct is in the first instance independent of its object; nor is its origin likely to be due to its object's attractions" (1905d, p. 148).

The theory of the instinct in relation to bisexuality

In short, "instinct", which is *Trieb* in German, will be better understood if referred to as "drive". In *Three Essays on the Theory of Sexuality*, Freud added few paragraphs dedicated to the concept of drive in 1915, and below is an extract from that. This is the most clear and useful definition among all other descriptions of drive by Freud.

> . . . the psychical representative of an endosomatic, continuously flowing source of stimulation, as contrasted with a "stimulus", which is set up by single excitations coming from without. The concept of instinct [drive] is thus one of those lying on the frontier between the mental and the physical . . . in itself an instinct is without quality, and, so far as the mental life is concerned, is only to be regarded as a measure of the demand made upon the mind for work. (1905d, p. 168)

Drive is, thus, a concept whose origin is neither solely the biological sphere nor the mental. It is located in between the body and the psyche. Which is why Freud referred to it as a "psychical representative" of the source of excitement, or "stimulation", arising from within the body. It is important to note that drive is a "representative", according to Freud in this comment, meaning that drive is a representation of something else. The presence of this *something else* is, although felt primarily in the manifestation of symptoms, remains out of reach and cannot be located or examined on its own using the conventional methods of examination. Drive is also to be understood as something that has no quality of its own and "is only to be regarded as a measure of the demand made upon the mind for work" (1905d, p. 168). Drive is different than other stimuli in the sense that its source is the "process of excitation occurring in an organ", which can be the "erotogenic zones" of the body, meaning the several orifices, such as eyes, mouth, nose, ears, and the genitals (1905d, p. 168). Finally, the aim of the drive, as described by Freud here, is "the removal of the organic stimulus" (1905d, p. 168). By using the term "erotogenic zone", Freud opened up the concept of sexuality from its narrow view of the usual genital heterosexual relations aimed only at reproduction.

"Object", on the other hand, has various meanings in psychoanalysis. For now, object in relation to the drive is to be understood as "the thing in regard to which or through which the instinct is able to achieve its aim" (Freud, 1915c, p. 122). The aim as Freud described it is "the act towards which the instinct tends" (1905d, p. 136). This object can be a real person or a certain aspect of this person, or an animal, or an inanimate object—the possibilities are endless. The object can also be an internal agency, such as the ego itself. However, it must be noted that not just any object will satisfy a certain drive; the object will vary from person to person. Objects are determined by the person's subjective history, especially their earliest history, which gives objects a subjective characteristic and, thus, objects that will satisfy a drive will always have highly distinct traits. As described above, Freud observed that when it comes to human sexuality, the bond between the sexual object and sexual aim is much looser than society or human civilisation would expect it to be and, rather, it is anything but predetermined.

For Freud, an instinct, or drive, is always active because it always has an aim (1905d, p. 219). This is because a drive is always seeking to remove the organic stimulus. Hence, for Freud, a drive is always masculine (mentioned in Chapter Three). Libido, which is the energy fuelling the drive, is always, according to Freud, "invariably and necessarily of a masculine nature, whether it occurs in men or in women and irrespective of whether its object is a man or a woman" (1905d, p. 219). This means that even when the drive has a passive aim, it is to be considered as masculine. Using this logic, the little girl's phallic activity, clitoral masturbation, is to be understood as masculine. Along the path of sexual development, and "the development of the inhibitions of sexuality (shame, disgust, pity etc.)", if the drive in her prefers a passive form, even then, psychoanalysis would consider her libido to be of masculine character. This is a much more reliable and concrete use of the terms masculine and feminine than the biological sense or the sociological sense.

This theory uses different parameters than Fleiss's theory of bisexuality, which depends somewhat on the biological sex of the person. However, Freud noted in *Civilization and Its Discontents* (1930a) that "the theory of bisexuality is still surrounded by many obscurities, and we cannot but feel it as a serious impediment in psychoanalysis that it has not yet found any link with the theory of the instincts" (1930a,

p. 106). This comment suggests that Freud rather regrets not having found the missing piece that would connect the two theories together. So, he speculated, and wrote that if one is to consider that "each individual seeks to satisfy both male and female wishes in his sexual life", then this will be in line with the theory of bisexual disposition (1930a, p. 106). However, the problem arises when one considers the possibility that "[two sets of] demands are not fulfilled by the same object", and that these drives will interfere with each other unless they are kept apart (1930a, p. 106), meaning that if one is to consider Fleiss's theory of bisexual deposition, then the drives with opposite sexual aim should not interfere, but, considering Freud's drive theory, it is highly likely that the drives *will* interfere with one another, which, in turn, contradicts Fleiss's bisexual disposition theory. This does not, however, negate the fact that Freud agrees with Fleiss regarding the importance and implications of the idea of bisexuality for the understanding of psychoanalysis, which is why Freud wrote,

> Since I have become acquainted with the notion of bisexuality I have regarded it as the decisive factor, and without taking bisexuality into account think it would scarcely be possible to arrive at an understanding of the sexual manifestations that are actually to be observed in men and women. (Freud, 1905d, p. 220)

Interestingly, in the next chapter, where we closely read "Femininity" (1933a, Lecture XXXIII), it is evident that the text again picks up on the very confusion that this chapter and the previous chapter have ended with. After all, masculine, feminine, male, and female are terms that, although seeming quite straightforward, pose fundamental questions for human beings. As we shall see in the next chapter, Freud will again begin his lecture by illustrating the very difficulty of separating and defining concepts such as masculine and feminine, even from purely scientific and biological perspectives.

CHAPTER FIVE

New Introductory Lectures on Psycho-analysis (1933a): Lecture XXXIII, "Femininity"

Introduction

S trachey (1933, p. 112) suggested that this particular lecture is based on two of Freud's earlier writings, "Some psychical consequences of the anatomical distinction between the sexes" (1925j) and "Female sexuality" (1931b). Both papers have been discussed in detail earlier in this book (see Chapters Two and Three). Hence, there is some repetition in this chapter of topics and arguments that we have already discussed, but, despite this, reading this chapter will allow us to grasp how Freud's arguments developed and what importance he now places, at this stage of his career, on the centrality of castration in the development of human sexuality.

This lecture appears in *New Introductory Lectures on Psycho-Analysis* (Freud, 1933a). However, in the winter terms of 1915–1916 and 1916–1917, Freud had already delivered a few lectures in the Vienna Psychiatric Clinic that are known as the *Introductory Lectures on Psycho-analysis*. So, the question is, what is so "new" or different about these lectures from the 1930s? In relation to this question, Freud, in the Preface for these lectures, mentioned the following. These lectures were never delivered, unlike the ones from the mid 1910s. Owing to a surgical operation, speaking in public became almost impossible for Freud (1933a, p. 5), but Freud continued delivering lectures in an unconventional way. He began to document his learning and findings in a lecture-like structure, "only by an artifice of the imagination; it may help me not to forget to bear the reader in mind as I enter more deeply into my subject" (Freud, 1933a, p. 5). Freud further urged his readers not to mistake these lectures as intended to replace the earlier ones, as they are not independent entities "with an expectation of finding a circle of readers of its own" (1933a, p. 5). Rather, these new lectures are intended as "continuations and supplements" to the earlier ones (1933a, p. 5). Some of them are critical revisions of subjects that were dealt with in the earlier series, some are true extensions of theories, and others consist of fresh material that did not exist at the time of the earlier ones. Lecture XXXIII, "Femininity", is a combination of all of these. Freud's main aim in these lectures, and especially in the lecture on "Femininity", was "to make no sacrifice to an appearance of being simple, complete or rounded-off, not to disguise problems and not to deny the existence of gaps and uncertainties" (1933a, p. 6). Such is the subject of "mental life", which will inevitably face the enquirer with sudden moments of uncertainty in his quest. Similarly, "throughout history people have knocked their heads against the riddle of the nature of femininity" (Freud, 1933a, p. 113). So far, this book has illustrated how such puzzlement is also evident throughout Freud's earlier writings, especially when it comes to formulating a rounded-off theory of the castration complex.

Defining sex

Freud starts by highlighting a mundane phenomenon from daily life. It might seem that every time we meet a new person, "with unhesitating certainty" we first make one quick distinction, "male or female?" (Freud, 1933a, p. 113). However, Freud questions the apparent anatomical certainty on which this quick distinction is based. This is because Freud agues that it only works up to a certain point and not beyond it. He again highlights that it is obvious that the spermatozoon, which is the male sex cell responsible for fertilising the ovum, is found only in males and the ovum, which is the female sex cell, is found only in females. However, in both sexes, the sex organs develop "from the same [innate] disposition into two different forms" (1933a, p. 113). This innate disposition has already been discussed in both Chapters Three and Four. Secondary sexual characteristics, such as body shapes, height, tissue, presence or absence of breasts, facial hair, Adam's apple, etc., usually develop at puberty and they can help to distinguish between the sexes but, unlike the sex organs, they are not directly involved in reproduction. Besides the sex organs, when it comes to these secondary sexual characteristics, it is evident that they are rather inconstant and they vary widely. This would suggest that using secondary sexual characteristics for the purposes of distinguishing between the sexes is not so reliable. Does that mean that a person's sex organ is the most reliable factor when it comes to making a quick decision about that person's anatomical gender (a term that is not used in Freudian vocabulary)? When it comes to the discipline of biological science, that might be the case. However, Freud draws our attention to the fact that, even in biology, there is something that runs counter to this expectation and it adds a drop of confusion to this apparent certainty. Freud writes, ". . . portions of the male sexual apparatus also appear in women's bodies, though in an atrophied state, and vice versa in the alternative case" (1933a, p. 114). This is something he had already highlighted in his previous texts.

He explains that science would regard these occurrences as "indications of *bisexuality*", meaning that a person is "not a man or woman but always both – merely a certain amount more the one than the other" (1933a, p. 114). This is a much clearer argument on Freud's part. This would suggest that one has to be familiar with the idea that not only is an individual a combination of masculine and feminine anatomical elements, but also that "the proportion in which masculine and feminine are mixed in an individual is subject to quite considerable fluctuations" (1933a, p. 114). When it comes to biology, the sexual products, such as ova or semen, are never present together in the same human except in very rare cases of hermaphroditism, where both sets of sex organs may be found, but in an atrophied condition. Freud questions the "decisive significance of those elements" which contribute towards the construction of an individual's sex and he concludes, "what constitutes masculinity or femininity is an unknown characteristic which anatomy cannot lay hold of" (1933a, p. 114). This is a distinctive comment on which psychoanalytic examinations are based. A psychoanalytic understanding of, and approach to, the subjects of sex, sexuality, and sexual identity are, thus, beyond anatomical investigation. Human sexuality is, thus, not a matter of biological facts but, rather, is to be investigated from the workings of the mental life of the person. Yet, the concept of this mental life is not to be equated with psychology. Why?

Freud questions how psychology helps us to understand these concepts. Often, we speak of mental qualities as "masculine" and "feminine". By assigning these terms to mental qualities, we tend to characterise the "mental life" of humans as bisexual (1933a, p. 114). For instance, despite his or her biological sex, one can speak of the same individual "behaving in a masculine way in one connection and in a feminine way in another" (1933a, p. 114). However, if these perceptions are examined, it would reveal that anatomy, or what is known as "convention", is being prioritised when one attempts to transfer the notion of bisexuality to human mental life or to someone's behaviour. The term "convention" is to be understood as an amalgam of the concepts of tradition, regularity, and typicality. Freud believes that one can never put a "new connotation" to the concepts of masculine and feminine, as it would always refer back to the anatomical sense, or social constructions, or societal norms. The distinction between these terms is, therefore, not psychological in nature. Freud acknowledges, in general, that the term "masculine" can have a connotation of "active" and "feminine" might be referred to as "passive". He examines this correlation and questions the "behaviour of the elementary sexual organisms" (1933a, p. 114). The male sex cell can be described as the active one, as it is mobile and it searches for the female sex cell, the ovum, which, in fact, is immobile, sits quietly, and "waits passively" (1933a, p. 114). Given the time of this text, it is understandable, albeit debatable, that Freud wrote "this behaviour of the elementary sexual organisms is indeed a model for the conduct of sexual individuals during intercourse" (1933a, p. 114).

Freud is a man of his time and this is evident in his following explanation. He said it is the male who "pursues the female for the purpose of sexual union, seizes hold of her and penetrates into her" (1933a, p. 114). But notice how he uses the term "male" and not "men". By using the term "male", he does not restrict himself to humans. It would be rather useful if one can hold off the temptation to get into an argument about Freud's personal ideas about the sexual roles in the 1930s, because Freud is building his argument to make a much bigger statement. He immediately highlights that, by considering this as a model to understand the concepts of "masculine" and "feminine" from a psychological perspective, one would, essentially. have to reduce the characteristics of masculinity to aggressiveness.

The problem becomes even bigger when one considers the fact that, in the animal kingdom, there are various species where the females are more aggressive, stronger, more mobile, or "active", than the males. This is evident, for example, in spiders. Moreover, the characteristics which a society in general will immediately consider as feminine, in other words, the usual gender roles that society tends to assign to the concept of femininity, such as nurturing and caring, does not always correlate with the female sex in the animal world. In fact, many species share their parental duties between the male and the female. This is evident in 90% of bird species, and in many other species one can notice that the males alone devote themselves to such duties. Hence, when it comes to understanding the concepts of "masculine" and "feminine", there is no value in using such a model that links these terms with the concepts of stronger and aggressive and weaker and nurturing. Even in the case of human sexual life, Freud argues that it is inadequate to make active coincide with masculine behaviour and passive with feminine. The example he gives next is highly unusual and simply thought provoking.

Very often, the mother's affectionate acts towards the child are associated with adjectives such as passive, nurturing, non-aggressive, and "feminine". Freud proposes the following. "A mother is active in every sense towards the child; the act of lactation itself may equally be described as the mother suckling the baby or as her being sucked by it" (Freud, 1933a, p. 115). This is a revolutionary proposal on various levels. While this comment might be interpreted as a point of view that has great scope for psychologically empowering or motivating women, from a psychoanalytic perspective, however, this comment reveals a great deal of other information which is extremely useful in understanding the human psyche, particularly that of a woman and her sexuality. With regard to a woman's psyche, one can question, is the very act of nursing the baby ever interpreted by the mother herself as active? Whether it *is* interpreted by the mother as such, at the level of her conscious mind, or it remains at the level of the unconscious, not intellectualised, either way, this piece of knowledge, this very interpretation of Freud's, affects the general perception of the dynamic of the mother–child relation. For Freud, it is not just an act of nurturing and love, there is a libidinal activity involved in this dynamic. In this sense, the mother's role in the care of the baby can be interpreted as an activity of the masculine libido. This perception of the "change in sex" (Freud, 1931b, p. 228) can be only perceived through the Freudian prism of the drive theory.

Further ,we can ask, is the woman aware of this knowledge from a very early age: that in suckling the baby she, as a mother, plays an active part? The answer is: maybe. This is because, in "Female sexuality" (1931b, p. 237), Freud described the little girl's play with her dolls and her request that her mummy should play a reversal of their roles as the girl's attempt to swing over from the position of passivity to activity. This theory can be interpreted as follows. The little girl, at a very young age, *might* perceive the act of feeding or nurturing or performing the caring chores that her mother "does *to* her", as an active thing. She *might* think that she, too, can reverse the roles and put someone else in the position of passivity, if she herself becomes a mother. The intensity and the fate of this wish depend on a multitude of other factors and they would also vary from individual to individual.

However, it becomes trickier to answer if we ask the question, "how"? How *does* this realisation, or perception, or knowledge of the woman that suckling or nurturing is an activity affect the dynamics of the mother–child relation? Does the child become an object of the mother on to which she expresses and exercises her activity? Something that provides her with reasons to feel empowered and liberated? Does the concept of the child, or the child himself, make up for all the passivity she once experienced as a child, from her own mother? What about the aggressiveness she experienced and the reproach she felt towards her mother, which Freud speaks of in this very text (1933a, p. 116)? According to Freud, the suppression of her aggressiveness influences the development of her "powerful masochistic impulses" (1933a, p. 116). Does the knowledge that suckling the baby is an activity affect these impulses? Considering that the child is often perceived by the mother as an extension of herself, which is biologically correct, as they are separated by the cutting of the umbilical cord after the birth of the baby, then can these masochistic impulses be directed towards the child, too?

Similar to the act of suckling, can we consider the directing of the masochistic impulses towards the child as active, a position of empowerment, a reversal of roles, or a swing-over from passivity to activity? Something that a woman might have known since a very young age and wished for? These are questions that can be raised and debated endlessly. However, psychoanalysis is about individuality and subjectivity and, hence, it is the individual negotiation of the threat or the discovery of castration that will be the key in determining the answer to this question as to *how* will the knowledge that suckling/nurturing the baby demonstrates activity affect the dynamics of the mother–child relationship for a particular person. For the moment, it is important to note that apparent feminine characteristics can reveal libidinal activities operating underneath. Since libido always has an aim, it is to be considered as masculine, and a mother's nurturing act can be perceived as masculine from a psychoanalytic perspective. Hence, concepts such as "masculine" and "feminine" are extremely difficult to comprehend and it would be a mistake to correlate these terms with activity and passivity based on "convention" (Freud's term, 1933a, p. 114). This is precisely what Freud is highlighting in this text. The further away we go from the "narrow sexual sphere", the more we will see that "women can display great activity in various directions" and that "men are not able to live in company with their own kind unless they adopt a large amount of passive adaptability" (Freud, 1933a, p. 115). However, if we are to draw a conclusion that, in a psychological sense, men and women are bisexual, it would only reflect that one has decided to link the term "passive" with "feminine" and "active" with "masculine" (Freud, 1933a, p. 115). Freud strongly advises us not to draw such a conclusion and, hence, it can be argued that psychological bisexuality is a concept that is not a very useful tool for examining psychosexual development.

If we were to characterise femininity psychologically, can we describe it as a position that gives "preference to passive aims" (Freud, 1933a, p. 115)? Freud argues that this position is not to be equated with passivity, because achieving a passive aim requires "a large amount of activity" (1933a, p. 115). From a social science perspective, it is absolutely valid to consider that the influence of social customs "force women into passive situations" (Freud, 1933a, p. 116). The limits, restrictions, and boundaries enforced on the woman from the very beginning of her life can be considered to influence her preference for passive aims and behaviours. In other words, Freud is speculating that a woman's sexual life could be considered as following the model of her life in general to some extent, shaped by the constraints put on her by society. However, from a psychoanalytic perspective, Freud notices one "constant relation between femininity and instinctual life" (1933a, p. 116). These demands made upon a woman, both constitutionally and socially, to suppress her aggressiveness influence the development of these "powerful masochistic impulses" that we mentioned earlier (Freud, 1933a, p. 116). Freud suggests that these impulses "erotically" bind "the destructive trends which have been diverted inwards" (1933a, p. 116).

Why did he use the term "erotically"? Is there any *other* way of binding impulses within the psychoanalytic context? If sexuality is the key to unlocking the mystery of all psychoneurosis, according to Freud, then can we *not* conclude that there is no other way that impulses are bound in our psyche except "erotically"? Can we then consider masochism as "truly feminine" (1933a, p. 116)? But what happens when we see masochism in men? Are we to make sense of masochism in men as instances of men exhibiting "very plain feminine traits" (1933a, p. 116)? This is where Freud emphasises that these instances of confusion highlight the limits of psychology: "psychology too is unable to solve the riddle of femininity" (1933a, p. 116). How else do we explain femininity? The very fact that, generally speaking, in living organisms, there exist differences in sex is a crucial point to note because the very "existence of two sexes is the most striking characteristic of organic life which distinguishes it sharply from inanimate nature" (1933a, p. 116). But how does "the differentiation of living organisms into two sexes come about" (1933a, p. 116)?

This is where Freud makes this crucial distinction between other schools of enquiry and a psychoanalytic enquiry into the question of femininity: "psychoanalysis does not describe what a woman is – that would be a task it could scarcely perform – but sets about enquiring how she comes into being, how a woman develops out of a child with a bisexual disposition" (1933a, p. 116). In essence, when it comes to the question of femininity, psychoanalysis prioritises the *construction* of femininity rather than its *definition*. A detailed discussion on Freud's position on the concept of "bisexual disposition", as mentioned in this comment, can be found in Chapter Four. At the heart of this *construction* of femininity lies castration and, in psychoanalysis, the acquisition of sexuality is a reaction to castration; it is a result of the individual negotiation of the Oedipus complex. Freud has, throughout his career, questioned the psychosexual development of a woman again and again, where, as a reaction to castration, he has mainly outlined the theories of penis envy. What does he propose in *this* text with regard to the theory of "the sexual development of women" (Freud, 1933a, p. 117)?

Rather different

Freud highlights two "expectations" with which he approaches the investigation into the question of "the sexual development of women":

> It is a path that includes struggle i.e. adapting to the demands of the constitution does not come without considerable amount of resistance and hence, sexual development of the woman is far from smooth-sailing; the decisive turning-points will already have been prepared for or completed before puberty. (Freud, 1933a, p. 117)

Compared to the boy's psychosexual development, the girl's development already seems more complex. The transformation of the "little girl into a normal woman" is comparatively more difficult as it follows a more complicated pathway than of the little boy, precisely because there are "two extra tasks, to which there is nothing corresponding in the development of a man" (1933a, p. 117). These "two extra tasks" in the previous essay, titled "Female sexuality" (1931b) referred to the exchange of the primacy of the clitoris for the vagina and the exchange of her first love-object, that is, turning away from her mother and choosing her father. A detailed discussion on this point can be found in Chapter Three. The term "normal woman" in this quote is to be interpreted as Freud referring to the woman as heterosexual and she represents, or represented, the majority of women during the nineteenth century and the early twentieth century. To begin with, physically, there are stark differences between the sexes. From the beginning of life, the boy and the girl have different genitals and this is usually accompanied by different secondary sexual characteristics around puberty. Freud also noted the differences in their instinctual disposition, which, in the case of the little girl, provide glimpses of her later characteristics of womanliness. He suggested that a little girl is usually "less aggressive, defiant and self-sufficient", her need to receive affection is greater than the little boy's, that she is more "dependent and pliant", and, probably because of her pliancy, she is more easily and quickly taught to control her bodily excrements (Freud, 1933a, p. 117). Freud is examining a commonly held belief that a little girl is more easily potty trained than the little boy (debatable, but agreeable to most parents). Instead of examining the validity of this common idea, it would be useful to follow the chain of thought that led Freud to make this comment and what else he is leading to. In Lecture XXXII, "Anxiety and instinctual life" (1933a, p. 100), Freud studies the "transformation of instinct" and, referring to Abraham's work, Freud highlights the following.

> ... after a person's own faeces, his excrements, has lost its value for him, this instinctual interest derived from the anal source passes over on to objects that can be presented as *gifts*. And this is rightly so, for faeces were the first gift that an infant could make, something he could part with out of love for whoever was looking after him. (Freud, 1933a, p. 100)

Urine and faeces are bodily productions, made by the children and given away at the adult's demand. The "pliancy" in this act of giving, or offering, or parting with something that one has produced oneself in order to please the other is one of the very first experiences of the child where he or she learns that giving or *not* giving invokes a reaction in the other. As adults, we "part with" our own production, that is, money we have earned, using our own labour, out of love for the other. Gifts are expression of love and this is why, in this current text, "Femininity", Freud again highlights that faeces and urine are the first gifts that, as humans, we give to the other who looks after us, "and controlling them is the first concession to which the instinctual life of children can be induced" (1933a, p. 117). This comment would suggest that, if we accept that a little girl's need to receive affection is stronger than the boy's, then her "first concession to which her instinctual life" is "induced" might provide valuable information in understanding the later erotic bindings of her instinctual life. However, as both the boy and the girl go through the routine of personal hygiene and both face the demand from the other who is responsible for looking after them with regard to their control of their bodily movements, the instinctual life of *both the little boy and the little girl* will be influenced by this "first concession", which is, Freud confirms, that both sexes pass through the "early phases of libidinal development" in a similar manner (1933a, p. 117).

Drawing on clinical observations of children and from other women analysts, Freud notes that there is no reason to believe that for the little girl there is less aggressiveness in her sadistic–anal phase. Very briefly, sadism within the psychoanalytic context is a concept that goes beyond the social and ideological understanding of the term. For Freud, sadism is "one of the fundamental components of instinctual life" (Laplanche & Pontalis, 1973, p. 400). This second stage of libidinal development in Freudian theory is the sadistic–anal phase, which usually occurs between the second and the fourth year of the child's life (Laplanche & Pontalis, 1973, p. 35). The chief erotogenic zone during this phase is the anus and the organisation of the libido during this stage occurs "under the primacy of anal erotogenic zone" (Laplanche & Pontalis, 1973, p. 35). The development of sadomasochism, within the psychoanalytic context, correlates with muscular control and, hence, knowledge of the sadistic–anal phase is invaluable in understanding the organisation of one's instinctual life.

The little girl is a little man

Freud explains that the difference between the sexes reduces further as the boy and the girl enter the phallic phase and he writes, "we are now obliged to recognize that the little girl is a little man" (Freud, 1933a, p. 118). (For a detailed discussion on the phallic phase, see Chapter Two.) During the phallic stage, both sexes derive pleasurable sensations from the genitals and masturbatory acts are carried out using the organs of the phallic zone: for boys it is the penis, and for girls it is the clitoris, the "penis-equivalent" (Freud, 1933a, p. 118). Freud believes that, at the phallic stage, the existence and functions of the feminine vagina are undiscovered by both sexes. Therefore, in the 1930s, as is demonstrated in "Female sexuality" (1931b), Freud maintains his position with regard to the clitoris of the little girl in her phallic stage as the "leading erotogenic zone", which is similar to his theories in the 1920s (Chapter Two). Now, however, Freud takes a stronger stance. He considers that from the position of this "little man", if the little girl is to achieve the development of femininity, the clitoris cannot remain as the chief erotogenic zone past the phallic stage. So Freud wrote, "with the change to femininity the clitoris should wholly or in part hand over its sensitivity, and at the same time its importance, to the vagina" (Freud, 1933b, p. 118). Handing over its sensitivity and importance from the clitoris to the vagina: this is one of the two extra tasks that a little girl has to perform for the development of her femininity, according to Freud in 1933. Compared to the little girl, the boy seems fortunate in this theory, because he "has only to continue at the time of his sexual maturity the activity that he has previously carried out at the period of the early efflorescence of his sexuality" (Freud, 1933b, p. 118). Here, in this comment, "activity" refers to the act of deriving pleasure from the male organ, the penis. This act related to his organ stays the same in the case of the boy, but for the girl, the choice of organ is to be different than before. What is the second task that the little girl has to perform on the way towards the development of femininity?

Organisation of the sexual instinct

To investigate the second task, as described in the current text, we must refresh our minds and revisit what Freud proposed about the development of instinctual life in his *Introductory Lectures on Psychoanalysis* (1916–1917). In Lecture XXI, "The development of libido" (1916–1917, pp. 328–329), Freud explained that the sexual life, that is, the libidinal function of a child, neither emerges as "ready-made" nor develops on its own accord. Rather, it is developed through a series of phases, repeating the course of development several times, similar to the transformation of a caterpillar into a butterfly (1916–1917, p. 328). Freud considered that "the turning-point" of this development was the phase where all components of the sexual instincts are organised under "the primacy of the genitals" and sexuality becomes subjected to reproductive function. In other words, the "turning-point" of psychosexual development described by Freud in 1917 is when a child's body becomes capable of reproduction and when all components of libido become organised under the primacy of the genitals (the penis in the boy and the vagina in the girl). Why is this an important aspect to highlight in this context? It is because Freud is trying to highlight the following notion. Before reaching this turning-point, the sexual life of the child is somewhat "distracted", unorganised, and involves "the independent activity of the different component instincts striving for organ-pleasure" (1916–1917, pp. 328–329). This is precisely how Freud described human sexuality from the beginning of human life in *Three Essays on the Theory of Sexuality* (1905d): "polymorphously perverse". From the beginning of life, the development of sexuality is influenced by relations between the components of the sexual instincts and their objects (Freud, 1916–1917, p. 328). Some components of sexual life will have an object from the very beginning and these objects will remain unchanged for a long time, such as the instinct of mastery in sadism and the instincts of scopophilia and epistemophilia in the enjoyment of looking and knowing, to name a few (1916–1917, p. 328).

Other components of the sexual instinct are more clearly attached to particular erotogenic zones of the body. To begin with, there is only one such link, which is the mouth and the act of suckling. As part of children's development, the component of the sexual instinct still remains attached to the "non-sexual functions" and they "give it up when they become separated from them" (1916–1917, p. 328). For instance, oral enjoyment is the first active component of the sexual instinct in the child's life. The first object of this oral component of the sexual instinct is the mother's breast. The infant's need for nourishment is satisfied by the breast. Both the need for nourishment and an erotic component is simultaneously satisfied in this act of suckling. With the course of the further development of instinctual life, this erotic component, "makes itself independent with the act of sensual sucking [*lutschen*]; it gives up the outside object and replaces it by an area of the subject's own body" (Freud 1916–1917, p. 329). This is evident when one witnesses a child sucking on its thumb and comforting itself. The phrase "subject's own body" here would refer to the child's thumb replacing the mother's breast. The oral instinct, thus, becomes "*auto-erotic*" (Freud, 1916–1917, p. 329).

From "little man" to little girl

Returning to the current text from 1933, we will now see that repeats the above point. Freud notes that, for both the little girl and the little boy, the mother is the first object of love. In the case of the boy, the mother remains the first love-object both during the formation of the boy's Oedipus complex and, in a sense, throughout his life. The various phases of the organisation of instinctual life occur in both sexes. Hence, the first "object-cathexes", as described above, also occur in both sexes where attachments to the satisfaction of bodily needs, such as nourishment and hygiene, take place (Freud, 1933a, p. 118). However, in the case of the little girl, she has to "pass from her mother to an attachment to her father" (Freud, 1933a, p. 119). This view is similar to that outlined in Freud's earlier paper, "Female sexuality" (Freud, 1931b) and it is also explained by Freud in more detail in his writings from 1923 to 1925. In other words, Freud's position in the 1930s remains that a girl has to "change her erotogenic zone and her object" for the development of her femininity, whereas the boy retains both his erotogenic zone and his object (Freud, 1933a, p. 119). Now Freud asks, how does the little girl pass from "her masculine phase" where the clitoris is her chief erotogenic zone and the mother is her love-object to the feminine phase "which she is biologically destined" to do (Freud, 1933a, p. 119).

Before delving deeper in search of the answer, it is worth noticing the choice of words Freud made in this last comment. Considering that the original text was written in German and that James Strachey, Freud's official translator, is responsible for this particular selection of words, the question still remains open as to what Freud means by "biologically destined"? Could it refer to vaginal intercourse and giving birth? Considering that Freud was a physician and the topic in hand refers to the primacy of the vagina in the development of femininity, it is quite possible that such is the case.

Freud teases his reader further by pointing out that it would be easier, ideal, and simplistic if one imagines that at some point in their lives the "elementary influence of the mutual attraction between the sexes" is felt by the little boy and he continues with his mother as his love-object (Freud, 1933a, p. 119) while the little girl is impelled by the same law of attraction and chooses her father as her love-object. One can also assume that these choices are influenced by parental choices, that the children "are following the pointer given them by the sexual preference of their parents" (Freud, 1933a, p. 119). Unfortunately, this is not a reliable explanation and, hence, Freud turns to his clinical observations. Freud notes that it is not unusual to know of cases where women have remained deeply dependent on a paternal object or even on their own father until a late age. But Freud discovered something very unusual about these intense and long attachments of women to their fathers, something he had already mentioned in his earlier text, "Female sexuality" (1931b). Analysis shows that everything that is revealed in the woman's relation to her father already existed in her earlier attachment to her mother and "it has been transferred subsequently on to her father" (Freud, 1933a, p. 119). Hence, once again in 1933, Freud highlights the importance of the girl's pre-oedipal phase and her attachment to her mother during this phase in understanding the development of femininity.

The nature of the little girl's libidinal relation to her mother will be of several and various kinds. This is because these libidinal relations pass through three phases of infantile sexuality. As they pass through these oral, anal, and phallic phases, they inherit characteristics of these phases and they "express themselves by oral, sadistic–anal and phallic wishes" (Freud, 1933a, p. 120). These wishes represent both active and passive impulses, and they are ambivalent in nature as they are both affectionate and hostile or aggressive in nature. For Freud these are "early sexual wishes", whose formulation is extremely difficult to point out (1933a, p. 120). However, Freud highlights various clinical considerations. For example, these hostile and aggressive wishes from the early stages of libidinal organisation can be discovered after they are "changed into anxiety ideas" (1933a, p. 120). For a detailed discussion on libidinal wishes and anxiety, see *Inhibitions, Symptoms and Anxiety* (Freud, 1926d). (This text has not been read closely in this book.) Moreover, the most clearly expressed wish during these early years "is a wish to get the mother with child and the corresponding wish to bear her a child" (Freud 1933a, p. 120). This is again a clear proposition that did not exist in this form in Freud's earlier papers. Freud believes that both these wishes belong to the phallic phase of the child's psychosexual development and they are established "beyond doubt by analytic observation" (1993a, p. 120). The detailed discovery of these findings in analysis are certainly surprising and worth noting. For example, at the very core of paranoiac illness, Freud discovered the fear of being murdered or poisoned, which was present already in relation to the mother during the child's pre-Oedipus phase.

Another example that Freud outlined here caused several controversies in Freud's career prior to this text. During 1895 and 1897,

Freud developed, and subsequently dropped, the theory of seduction, which aimed at "discovering infantile sexual trauma" (Freud, 1933a, p. 120). For the purposes of this book, we shall only continue with the current text as it unfolds. During this period, while Freud was examining memories of seduction in most of his female patients, the accounts given were that the subjects had been seduced by their fathers at an early stage of their lives. Freud later came to recognise that these reports were not true and that "hysterical symptoms are derived from phantasies and not from real occurrences" (Freud, 1933a, p. 120). Understandably, such a conclusion from Freud caused a lot of commotion. However, Freud now repeats that he recognised the following later. "The typical Oedipus complex in women" finds its expression in these phantasies of being seduced by the father (Freud, 1933a, p. 120). Furthermore, these phantasies are typically found in the pre-oedipal history of the woman, and the seducer here is the mother. This is in line with the fact that it is usually the mother who is in charge of helping the child with his or her hygiene routine and bodily needs, and Freud suggests that it is quite possible that these mundane chores probably stimulated or aroused the little child at some point, resulting in pleasurable sensations being felt by the child. This is a very similar account to that which Freud outlined in "Female sexuality" (1931b, p. 238).

Such a portrayal of the girl's Oedipus complex and the importance placed by Freud on her early sexual relations with her mother raise various issues and questions, and the reliability of such theories can be debated endlessly. Are these behaviours really noticeable in a little girl? Anticipating such a response from his readers, Freud reminds us that, while one might not agree with these views based on their regular observation of little girls, "enough can be seen in children if one knows how to look" (Freud, 1933a, p. 121). The tender and unsophisticated psyche of a child is able to bring very little of her experiences to her preconscious and it is hardly ever communicated at all. Because of that, Freud suggests that the investigation should rely on retrospectively studying the residues and repercussions of the early emotional world of people in whom these developments have left noticeable imprints. This is why he wrote that "pathology has always done us the service of making discernible by isolation and exaggeration conditions which would remain concealed in normal state" (Freud, 1933a, p. 121). Again, it is evident in this comment that, for

Freud, the difference in pathologies is a difference in degree and not in kind. Moreover, Freud justified the reliability of his theories by adding that even when he carried out such investigations on women who were by no means "seriously abnormal", the discovery was in no way different than his proposed theory (Freud, 1933a, p. 121).

Next, Freud examines the steps that lead to the end of this pre-oedipal attachment of the child to her mother. How does this intense and powerful attachment come to an end? Similar to his earlier text, "Female sexuality" (1931b), Freud again points out that the girl's turning away from her mother is not to be understood as a mere change in object. Her turning away is accompanied by hostility. In other words, Freud is suggesting again that the little girl's attachment to her mother ends in hatred and she turns away from the mother towards the father-object accompanied by the feeling of hostility. Freud stresses that this hostility could persist all through the woman's life, might be overcompensated for at some stage, and might also be partially overcome while another part of it might continue to persist. However, for the purpose of the investigation currently in hand, the focus should remain on the time she turns away from her mother and the motives that influence this turning away. The three key motives that Freud outlines are as follows: the child's reproaches to the mother rely on her feeling of not receiving enough nourishment, not enough affection, and the frustration the child feels due to the mother's interference with her pleasurable activity.

Not enough milk

This reproach goes back the furthest, where the child considers that she was not sufficiently nourished. This is regarded by the child as a sign of a lack of love. Whether historically this accusation is true or not, the importance lies in the issue that the child experiences it and regards it as a sign of lack of love. To Freud, it seems that the child has a keen attachment to, and an insatiable need for, her nourishment, which is why the child "never gets over the pain of losing its mother's breast" (Freud, 1933a, p. 122). Freud believes that this is because analysis with a child who has been given the maximum time at the breast, for example, even after the child has learnt to run and talk, will also reveal the same reason to reproach the mother. Freud further indicates that in cases where there is a fear of being poisoned, analysis can reveal its connection to the withdrawal of the breast. This is because "poison is nourishment that makes one ill" (Freud, 1933a, p. 122). Children possibly connect their early illnesses to this frustration, too. Freud notices that children, uneducated people, and primitive people do not possess the prerequisite intellectual education to make sense of phenomena and events (1933a, p. 122). It is quite possible that these people will assign a ground for any event without sophisticated, logical, intellectual consideration. So, he draws from both the social world and his clinic, and notes that, even today,

> . . . no one can die without having been killed by some else – preferably by the doctor . . . regular reaction of a neurotic to the death of someone closely connected with him is to put the blame on himself for having caused the death. (Freud, 1933a, p. 122).

Not enough affection

This accusation finds expression especially around the arrival of a new baby. The previous frustration felt about oral nourishment now flares up further as the child possibly makes sense of the situation in the following way: the mother is preserving the nourishment for the new arrival. This is particularly difficult if the children are very close in age; for example, this will be the case if they are eleven months apart. But the important thing to remember here is the fact that the child does not just begrudge the new arrival suckling at the breast but also *all the other maternal care* directed to the new baby. Freud believes that the child feels that she has been "dethroned, despoiled, prejudiced in its rights" (Freud, 1933a, p. 123). So, the child begins to feel jealous of the new arrival and the development of "grievance against the faithless mother" is set in motion (1933a, p. 123). Such a change in the behaviour of the mother simply seems disagreeable and unacceptable to the child. The child might begin to be "naughty", "irritable", "disobedient", and might even give up the control she has recently learnt over her excretions (1933a, p. 123). These are self-evident facts that have been, and can be, observed everywhere. However, it is rare that importance is attached to these events. Hardly anyone puts these pieces together and examines the "strengths of these jealous impulses, of the tenacity with which they persist and of the magnitude of their influence on later development" (Freud, 1933a,

p. 123). This is why Freud noted earlier that much can be seen in children, if only one knows where to look (Freud, 1933a, p. 121). This jealousy of the child is constant and it increases with each new arrival in the family. The sustainment of this jealousy and reproach is also independent of the factual reality that the child might be considered by the mother to be her favourite. Factual reality is quite different than one's psychic or internal reality and, hence, the internal consequences are independent of the external occurrence. Moreover, Freud highlighted that a child demands unconditional, endless, and immoderate love; he or she claims exclusivity and tolerates no sharing whatsoever. This would mean that no matter what the circumstances were or how the mother behaved, it would never be enough for the child; the attachment is bound to end in disappointment. This is, again, very similar to Freud's previous explanation outlined in "Female sexuality" (1931b).

Interference with pleasurable activity

The child's libido will never be fully satisfied. Yet, the various sexual wishes continue to alter as they pass through the various phases of libidinal organisation and sustain themselves by the growing hostility that the child feels towards the mother. During the phallic period, the child experiences the strongest of these frustrations when the mother forbids the child from pleasurable activity related to the genitals. This interference is often accompanied by severe threats and strong signs of disapproval. As mentioned before, daily mundane hygiene routine could introduce the child to sudden pleasurable feelings arising from his or her genitals. To the child, the mother is the seducer, the one who introduced the child to such activity. Now, it is the same mother who cruelly forbids the child such activity.

Doomed to dissolution

The reasons given above will seem sufficiently frustrating for the child to turn away from the mother. It also seems that infantile sexual wishes, the extreme characteristics of the infantile demand for love, and the impossibility of the fulfilment of their sexual wishes are responsible for a possible estrangement. One can consider that precisely because it is the child's first love-relation, it is destined to fail.

This early "object-cathexis", as Freud calls it, is highly ambivalent and, hence, the powerful tendency to aggressiveness coincides with a powerful love. As a result, the more passionately the child loves her object, the more sensitive she becomes to the disappointments and frustrations caused by the object. In the end, the destruction of the child's love for the mother is inevitable, despite the mildest and kindest upbringing, suggests Freud. However, if we were to consider that the frustrations and disappointments the child experiences in relation to the "love, the jealousy, the seduction followed by prohibition", were also felt by the little boy in his early life, then how come these factors did not detach the little boy from his mother? If only Freud could discover a "specific factor" (Freud, 1933a, p. 124) that operates in the case of the little girl but is absent, or does not operate in the similar way, in the case of the boy. How else do we explain the termination of the girl's intense attachment to her mother, unlike the boy under similar circumstances? Freud believes that this specific factor is found in the castration complex.

Reproach for being castrated

"After all, the anatomical distinction [between the sexes] must express itself in psychical consequences" (Freud, 1933a, p. 124). We have already learnt that the entire text "Some psychical consequences of the anatomical distinction between the sexes" (Freud, 1925j) was, in fact, exactly what the the title suggests and once again the same message is evident in this comment made by Freud in 1933. Freud had already alluded, in 1925, to the notion that the little girl feels that she has been wronged by her mother and now, in 1933, Freud builds his argument to support his previous view. He notes that little girls hold their mothers responsible for "their lack of a penis and do not forgive her for their being thus put at a disadvantage" (Freud, 1933a, p. 124). Although this would mean that both the little boy and the little girl are ascribed castration complex by Freud, it must be highlighted that the contents of this complex are anything but identical. For the boy, castration complex begins with the first sight of the female genital. The boy suddenly discovers that an organ so dear and valuable to him is not present in the girl's body. He recalls the threats made to him in relation to him enjoying his organ. The threats now seem much more believable than they were initially. He begins to fear castration and this becomes the most powerful motive force for his subsequent development (Freud, 1933a, p. 125). The little girl's castration complex also begins with her accidental sighting of the male genital. The difference and the significance are both noticed by the girl at once. Freud believes that the little girl feels "wronged", that she, too, wants something similar, and thus she falls "a victim to 'envy for the penis'" (Freud, 1933a, p. 125).

All of these occurrences leave everlasting imprints on the psyche of little girls and influence their future development, the "formation of their character", and cannot be overcome "without a severe expenditure of psychical energy" (Freud, 1933a, p. 125). Such an interpretation by Freud of feminine psychosexual development created, and continues to generate, a considerable amount of debate that is both scholarly and lay in nature. Freud himself included some of his critics' perspectives in "Female sexuality" (1931b, pp. 240–243); this is discussed in Chapter Three of this book. For the moment, it would be beneficial to continue with the text in order to discover what it is that Freud is alluding to and how this knowledge is useful for our understanding of human sexuality. Freud continues to explain that the little girl does not submit too easily to this fact that she is "without a penis" (Freud, 1933a, p. 125). Drawing on analytic observation, Freud suggests the following. The girl might develop a wish to receive something similar to what she sees is missing at some time in the future. She might continue to hope this way for many years, defying the knowledge of reality, rejecting the idea that the fulfilment of this wish is "unattainable", and her wish will be preserved in the unconscious (Freud, 1933a, p. 125). The next few lines of the text are more intriguing, as this is where one begins to grasp the relevance of this knowledge, not only in the clinic, but also in our everyday lives.

> The wish to get the longed-for penis eventually in spite of everything may contribute to the motives that drive a mature woman to analysis, and what she may reasonably expect from analysis – a capacity, for instance, to carry on an intellectual profession – may often be recognized as a sublimated modification of this repressed wish. (Freud, 1933a, p. 125)

Psychoanalytic activity is not something that can be handled like a pair of glasses that one puts on for reading and takes off when done (Freud, 1933a, p. 153). This is why the questions it evokes within us while reading Freud must be examined in a manner that is psychoanalytically informed and not governed by the compasses of ideology, morality, sense of entitlement, or sense of equality. Each of these compasses provides valuable theoretical and practical tools at very many levels, but none of them is psychoanalytic, none of them deals with the mental life of human beings, the mental life that is anything but ideal, moral, or equal. The workings of mental life are bound to contradict, surprise, confuse, perplex, and catch us off guard. Hence, it is worth questioning the following with a mind that is psychoanalytically informed and relatively free from any other predetermined biases. Can we perceive the "intellectual profession" chosen by a woman as a "sublimated modification" of her "repressed wish" for something she lacks but that others have? Is this something to be considered as the penis only, or, rather, what the penis represents? If we do not agree with Freud's perspectives, then from what examples or perspectives are *we* drawing that conclusion? The evaluation of both our agreement and disagreement must be psychoanalytically informed. We must question what our response tells us about ourselves and our own mental lives. If one is to engage with psychoanalytic literature, these moments of reflection are necessary, as they will prepare a fertile ground for future creation. Perhaps these reflections will "drive" one to analysis, as Freud proposed in his provocative comment as to where these questions can be further reflected upon.

Penis envy as a reaction to castration

Freud highlights the importance of penis envy and notes that his comments could have the potential to be taken as an instance of "male-injustice" (Freud, 1933a, p. 125). What he now proposes is that jealousy and envy play a much more important role "in the mental life of a woman than of men" (1933a, p. 125). This does not equate to the idea that men are incapable of possessing or displaying these two emotions, or that there are no other roots in women for these emotions than in relation to the absence of the penis. Rather, Freud is inclined to believe, from his clinical observations, that the presence of these emotions in women are greater than in men, and that a possible explanation for this *is* the absence of a penis which influences this production of envy.

Unlike other analysts of his time, Freud considers this "first-instalment of penis-envy" from the phallic phase as extremely important. Freud highlights a general problem of "depth-psychology" and states that he does not agree with analysts who are inclined to think that penis envy in women is a secondary structure which is evoked in times of "later conflicts" and that it is, rather, a regression to an earlier "infantile impulse" (Freud, 1933a, p. 126). According to Freud, depth psychology often questions pathological or unusual "instinctual attitudes" in a certain way. It can be viewed as a question of nature *vs.* nurture, the age-old debate that seldom comes to a satisfying conclusion for all. For instance, with regard to the aetiology of sexual perversion, depth psychology might ask the following: how much of the subject's "early infantile fixations" is to be considered as the influencing factor in the development of perversion and how much of the subject's later developments and experiences are to be considered as influencing the same (Freud, 1933a, p. 126)?

Complemental relation

In *Introductory Lectures on Psycho-analysis*, Lecture XXII (1916–1917), Freud discussed this issue in the following way. Attempting to distinguish neurotic illnesses based on their causation would lead to the creation of a series where the two factors, one's sexual constitution or fixation of the libido and one's experience of their frustration, would be represented in this way: "if there is more of the one there is less of the other" (Freud, 1916–1917, p. 347). Freud described this series as a "complemental series" (1916–1917, p. 347). At each extreme end of this series will be cases that are predominantly caused by one of the two factors mentioned above. For example, one extreme end of this series would feature a case where the subject's sexual experiences of childhood (i.e., traumatic external experiences leading to incomplete development) are predominately the cause of his neurosis, and, at the other extreme end of the series, would have the subject's sexual constitution (i.e., their fixation of libido) predominately influencing the development of neurosis. In between these two extreme poles we can imagine cases varying in degree where both of these factors are influencing the development of neurosis. When Freud refers to the fixation of libido in relation to the aetiology of neurosis, he is referring to (1) a constitutional factor which is made up of the subject's prehistoric experience (i.e., the subject's inherited constitution that presents them with various dispositions) and (2) the subject's infantile experience, which is not to be mistaken for traumatic experiences caused by adults to the child. Infantile experience is the child's internal experience, something that the child experiences on her own, irrespective of how the external reality was around her (i.e., the disposition acquired by the child during her early childhood) (Freud, 1916–1917, p. 362). It would be useful to imagine the fixation of libido as another "complemental series" made up of dispositions acquired from (1) prehistoric experiences and (2) infantile experience (1916–1917, p. 362).

With regard to "regression", if we consider the complemental relation that Freud outlined in 1917 "between the intensity and pathogenic importance" of one's infantile experience and one's later experiences, the two poles will be as follows. On the one hand, there will be cases that are predominantly influenced by the subject's "developmental inhibition" (i.e., cases where infantile sexual experience left impressions that can be traumatic), leading to an incomplete sexual development and a certain sexual constitution. On the other hand, there will be extreme cases of "regression", where later experiences of the subject predominately influenced the development of neurosis and, in analysis, the subject's impression of his childhood will be revealed as similar to what he has regressed to (Freud, 1916–1917, p. 364). Freud, thus, left the following question open: if a striking libidinal regression takes place, would it not be wiser to consider that hereditary constitution may *not* be the predominant factor here (1916–1917, p. 364)? In short, in 1917, Freud seemed to agree the following.

1.   In terms of the aetiology of neurosis, broadly speaking, there is a complemental relation between infantile experiences and later experiences.
2.   Regression seems to be in a complemental relation with developmental inhibition.
3.   With regard to fixation of libido, there is a further complemental relation between prehistoric disposition and dispositions acquired during early childhood.

In 1933, within the current text, Freud again returns to this subject in relation to the problem of depth psychology describing penis envy as a secondary formation where a subject regresses to early infantile impulses (Freud, 1933a, p. 126). He reminds the reader of his theory of the complemental series and repeats that early infantile fixations and later experiences are both factors that play a part in the causation of neurosis, but in varying amounts, "a less on the one side is balanced by a more on the other" (1933a, p. 126). Although the infantile factor influences the patterns in every case and it mostly determines the issues, too, that is not always the case; there are exceptions. However, in the case of penis envy, Freud argues that the infantile factor plays a crucial role in both setting the patterns and determining the issues (1933a, p. 126). The discovery that she is castrated is a major "turning-point" in the little girl's psychosexual developmental route. From here, there are three possible lines of development: (1) sexual inhibition or neurosis, (2) a change of character or a masculinity complex, and (3) normal femininity. Compared to the other appearances of Freud's theory on these three lines of psychosexual development of the little girl, this 1933 version is a much more developed and yet controversial one.

On the way to neurosis

According to Freud, the little girl has been living in a "masculine way" before she discovered the difference between the sexes; she has been deriving pleasure from clitoral masturbation, and she has been directing her sexual wishes towards her mother related to this enjoyment (Freud, 1933a, p. 126). As discussed above, these sexual wishes are not to be considered as passive, as they are active in every sense. After she discovers that she is "castrated", meaning she is without a penis, the development of "penis-envy" in her influences her to lose "enjoyment in her phallic sexuality" (Freud, 1933a, p. 126). The comparison to the "boy's far superior equipment" damages her "self-love" and it leaves her feeling mortified (1933a, p. 126). All of this leads to the little girl's renunciation of her clitoral masturbation. She develops dissatisfaction with such activity, and while she gives up her love for her mother, she also represses a large amount of her "sexual trends in general" (1933a, p. 126). It is important to note the terms used by Freud in relation to the girl's turning away from her mother. If the quoted terms seem strong, it is worth questioning, from a psychoanalytic perspective, as to why they seem so. One of the major reasons behind Freud's word selection shown above is that, according to Freud, the turning away from the mother is not just a mere change of object; the element of hostility accompanying this change in her object is crucial to notice. The intensity of this hostility will be undermined if the humiliation experienced by the little girl is not adequately captured in these texts. It would also be a mistake to consider this turning away of the little girl as one single act occurring on a particular day and particular time of her life. Rather, this is a gradual process that begins with the little girl considering her "castration as an individual misfortune", then slowly this theory is extended to the other females around her, and, finally, she begins to realise that even her mother is castrated (Freud, 1933a, p. 1 26). The little girl's love was directed towards her "phallic" mother, that is, the mother *with* a phallus (1933a, p. 126). But now, as the mother is regarded as someone *without* a phallus, someone who is just as unfortunate as herself in having been subjected to castration, "it becomes possible to drop her as an object", and this is how all the "motives for hostility" that have been operating for a long time now take over (Freud, 1933a, p. 126). This is a far more distinct and much clearer theorisation than Freud's earlier work.

So far, this theory explains that the girl's turning away from her mother is a gradual process which is accompanied by a strong feeling of hostility and that, in this process, the girl finally recognises that not only she herself, but women in general and one woman in particular, her mother, are castrated. Yet, how do we make sense of this following comment? Freud writes that the discovery of "women's lack of a penis" leads to women being "debased in value for girls just as they are for boys and later perhaps for men" (Freud, 1933a, p. 127). In a world where gender equality and women's rights are terms that we are far more familiar with than ever before in human history, there still exist detestable phenomena such as sexual discrimination, social restriction, gender pay gap, professional obstacles, sexual violence, and domestic violence, to name but few. It is as if a fundamental piece of knowledge is missing from the human mind which leads to a particular kind of ignorance. No matter how many publications, conferences, protests, drafting of policies, and through various other civilised media the word is spread, the message just does not seem to get across. Somehow, to some people, including women themselves, whatever their race, religion, culture, or academic background, it always seems that women are inherently lacking something. In the light of this disconcerting reality, how are we to make sense of Freud's comment?

Returning to the text, Freud further explains that "masturbation is the executive agent of infantile sexuality", and that it is the "faulty development" of infantile sexuality that leads to the development of neurosis (Freud, 1933a, p. 127). But Freud is not referring to the masturbation of the puberty period that patients often hold responsible for their adult sufferings and consider as their aetiology of neurosis. The real question, Freud believes, should be around the masturbatory act of the early infancy period. Freud strongly believed that "all factual details of early masturbation" are essential in understanding an individual's neurosis and his character (Freud, 1933a, p. 127), ". . . whether or not it was discovered, how the parents struggled against it or permitted it, or whether he succeeded in suppressing it himself. All of this leaves permanent traces on his development".

The male pronouns used in these comments should not restrict its content to one sex only. The importance placed on infantile masturbation and its factual details are equally valid in the case of the little girl and in the development of her neurosis. Freud provides a clinical example of a female patient who herself tried to "get free from masturbating" and did not succeed (1933a, p. 127). Envy for the penis usually provokes a strong impulse against "clitoridal masturbation", but if this impulse fails to override the wish to continue, the girl experiences a "violent struggle for liberation" (Freud, 1933a, p. 127). It is as if she becomes her own mother and, in order to withhold deriving pleasure from clitoral masturbation, she regards her dissatisfaction as being due to the inferiority of the organ (1933a, p. 127). Right into her adulthood, when her masturbatory activity is well suppressed, her interest continues to persist. Freud explains that the expression of this interest is often shown as sympathy for those whose sufferings are perceived as similar by our subject. The examples highlighted next are unlikely to seem foreign or far-fetched, even after almost a century. Freud considers that it plays a motive force behind "contracting a marriage", and might even "determine the choice of a husband or lover" (Freud, 1933a, p. 128). Freud recognises it as a "defence against temptation that is still dreaded" (i.e., defending a temptation to indulge in clitoral masturbation).

Before moving on, it is worth noticing that Freudian texts use the term "clitoridal" instead of "clitoral". To be precise, it is James Strachey, the translator, who uses this term in English, and not Freud. One possible reason for Strachey's use of "clitoridal" instead of "clitoral" is that the former refers to an act or object related to the clitoris, while the latter refers to the organ itself. It can be construed that this is what Freud meant, an enjoyment related to the clitoris, but did not specify this act as a direct enjoyment of the organ, the clitoris itself. Hence, the meaning of clitoral enjoyment in this text is to be understood as what Freud meant, an enjoyment related to the organ, the clitoris, but not an enjoyment of the organ itself.

The pathway to "normal"-ity

"If too much is not lost in the course of it through repression, this femininity may turn out to be normal" (Freud, 1933a, p. 128).

When the little girl abandons her clitoral masturbation, passivity triumphs over her previous position of activity. The "passive instinctual impulses" within her make it possible for the little girl to turn towards her father (Freud, 1933a, p. 128). In essence, this change in the nature of her instinctual impulses helps her to discard her phallic activity and prepare the ground for the development of femininity (1933a, p. 128). The little girl wished for a penis from her mother; feeling mortified and betrayed by her, she now turns to her father for the same. Freud explains that, in order for the feminine situation to be established, the original wish for the penis has to be sustained during this change of object, survive the mechanism of repression, and be replaced by the wish for a baby. During her phallic phase, the little girl did wish for a baby, while she played with her doll. But such a sight is not to be mistaken for her expression of femininity. As Freud had revealed before, the child's play with her doll was an expression of the little girl's "identification with her mother", an expression of her wish to *do to* the doll, what was *done to* her, an expression of her "intention of substituting activity for passivity" (Freud, 1933a, p. 128). In her play, she became the mother and the doll became her, but only when she begins to wish for a penis (i.e., only when she realises she is castrated) "the doll-baby" becomes a "baby from the girl's father" (Freud, 1933a, p. 128). This, according to Freud, is the most powerful feminine wish. This wish is fulfilled in the future when she does become a mother, and especially "if the baby is a little boy who brings the longed-for penis with him" (Freud, 1933a, p. 128). In her wish for "'a baby from her father'", the emphasis is on the baby and, hence, in this most feminine wish, one can find the expression of her "masculine wish for the possession of a penis", if only one knows how to look (Freud, 1933a, p. 128). Thus, Freud argues that the wish for a penis is probably the most feminine of all.

As we can see, it is castration that reminds the little girl of her lack of a penis, which drives her gradually away from her mother and influences her to turn towards the father. Her wish for a penis now becomes a wish for the penis-baby and, thus, she enters the Oedipus complex. The previously brewed hostility towards her mother now intensifies more than ever as the little girl begins to see her mother as her rival—a rival who received all that the little girl desires from her father, particularly a baby. For the little girl, the castration complex influences her entry into the Oedipus complex; the oedipal situation is, thus, an "outcome of a long and difficult development", it is a "preliminary solution" and a "position of rest" which the little girl does not abandon soon (Freud, 1933a, p. 129). At this stage, Freud returns to the issue he had in 1925 (see Chapter Two) and restates a remarkable difference between the sexes with regard to the "relation of the Oedipus complex to the castration complex" (Freud, 1933a, p. 129).

In the case of the little boy, he develops a rivalry with his father, wishes to get rid of him, and desires his mother naturally from his phallic phase. The threat of castration compels him to give up this position and, with the fear of losing his penis, he gets out of his Oedipus complex. In most non-pathological cases, he not only represses his wish for his mother, his Oedipus complex is destroyed completely and a "severe super-ego is set up as its heir" (Freud, 1933a, p. 129). In the case of the little girl, we see a complete opposite of this scenario. The castration complex does not destroy the girl's Oedipus complex; rather, it *prepares her for* her Oedipus complex. The envy of the penis influences the detachment of the girl from her mother and she enters the Oedipus complex wishing for a penis-baby from her father. The little girl faces no fear of castration and, hence, the prime motive for abandoning the oedipal situation does not exist for the little girl, unlike the little boy. Freud explains that the little girl stays in her Oedipus complex for considerably lengthy period of time and even when she does destroy her Oedipus complex, it is often done "incompletely" (Freud, 1933a, p. 129). This will indicate that the superego formation in women suffers a great deal as the circumstances are not really favourable for such development. This is why Freud asserts again, similar to his 1925 comment (see Chapter Two) that the superego in women "cannot attain the strength and independence which give it its cultural significance, and the feminists are not pleased when we point out to them the effects of this factor upon the average feminine character" (Freud, 1933a, p. 129).

The pathway to the masculinity complex

The reaction to the discovery of female castration might also influence the possible development of a "powerful masculinity complex" (Freud, 1933a, p. 129). For Freud, the development of this complex is usually led by the girl's refusal to admit that she is castrated. She becomes unsubmissive, rebellious, and might even begin to exaggerate her previous masculine position that belongs to the period before her discovery of castration (i.e., the knowledge that women do not have a penis). She refuses to give up her "clitoridal activity" and begins to identify with either her phallic mother or her father, both of whom are perceived by the little girl as being *not* castrated. Such a reaction to castration might be due to the little girl's "constitutional factor", which could be an excessive amount of "activity", which is "ordinarily characteristic of a male" (Freud, 1933a, p. 130). The constitutional factor, as we explained above, is the subject's various dispositions developed under the influence of her prehistoric experience and her infantile experience. As Freud notes, there is a clear avoidance of passivity that could lead to the development of femininity.

For Freud, the extremity of the masculinity complex will influence the choice of object and this might manifest as homosexuality. However, drawing from clinical observation, Freud clarifies that female homosexuality "is seldom or never a direct continuation of infantile masculinity" (Freud, 1933a, p. 130). Even when a girl follows the pathway to the development of her masculinity complex, she *does* take her father as an object briefly and *does* enter the Oedipus complex (1933a, p. 130), but, rather, it is the "disappointments from her father" that influence her regression to her early masculinity (1933a, p. 130). A girl who is "destined to become feminine" also faces similar disappointments from her father but the effect on her is not the same (Freud, 1933a, p. 130). What does Freud mean by "destined to become feminine"? Are we to consider the concept of femininity to be situated somewhere along the "complemental series", leaning towards the pole of the "constitutional factor" predominating over the development of the subject's character or neurosis? That could be true, because, in the case of female homosexuality, Freud agrees that "the predominance of the constitutional factor seems indisputable" (Freud, 1933a, p. 130). Are we assuming that "destined to be" equates with the person's sexual dispositions acquired prehistorically or during early childhood? To repeat, the "constitutional factor" is a combination of prehistoric disposition and infantile experience (i.e., dispositions acquired in early childhood).

Freud also highlights the notion that the practices of female homosexuality mirror the two phases of development: (1) the pre-oedipal mother–child dynamic and (2) the oedipal situation, that is, the child taking her father as an object temporarily. According to Freud, this is evident in female homosexual relations where partners "play the parts of mother and baby with each other as often and as clearly as those of husband and wife" (Freud, 1933a, p. 130). This would suggest that Freud's previous assertion is valid: female homosexuality is almost "never a direct continuation of infantile masculinity" (Freud, 1933a, p. 130). If it was a direct continuation of the child's masculinity complex belonging to the phallic phase, that is, the period *before* her discovery of castration, then how do we explain the two phases of development that Freud observes being mirrored in homosexual relationships? Freud's observation indicates, rather, that the little girl's masculinity complex must have gone through modification at several stages and, at times, it might even have been under the temporary influence of femininity. In other words, the child must have gone through the phases of the pre-oedipal attachment with the mother and, later, temporarily have chosen her father as an object before moving on elsewhere. This is one possible explanation of Freud's revelation that these two phases of development are mirrored in homosexual relationships, and this is why female homosexuality is never a direct continuation of the child's infantile masculinity within Freudian theories.

If we were to pause and reflect on the proposition made by Freud that the predominant factor in homosexuality is the constitutional factor, then it refers not just to the subject's disposition acquired from his or her prehistoric experience, but also the disposition acquired from their infantile experience (Freud, 1916–1917, p. 362). In other words, it is evident from our reading so far that, within the context of Freudian doctrine, it is much more than just what a child comes into this world *with* that makes them who they *are*. If that *is* the case, then it is probably wiser to question more than the layers and the sources of our behavioural make-up, down to the finer threads of our subjective positions, the motives behind our choice of objects, and particularly *how* they are influenced by the workings of our psyche. That would involve laborious work, inquisitiveness, a craving for knowledge, and an overall atmosphere around us that supports and encourages the formulation of a question within us *about us*. Rather, it would seem to be far more convenient to sing along with Lady Gaga and accept, "I was born this way". While there is a story in each of us of how we *came to be*, we are far more inclined to describe who we *are*; at least, such is true when it comes to our sexuality. Even in instances when investigations into ourselves about our sexuality are conducted, the paths followed are mostly of social science or biology or psychology. It is psychoanalysis that places the emphasis on mental life, but can we tolerate questioning the influences of our psyche on our sexual make-up? Does our society encourage such an appetite for knowledge? Do we reside in a society where questions about our subjectivity are allowed to be formed, supported, and nourished?

Those who have been there, done that: female analysts

Everything that has been discussed so far in this text by Freud is based on clinical observation made by both Freud himself and other clinicians. Freud suggests that, given the content of this text, it can be referred to as the "prehistory of women" (Freud, 1933a, p. 130). This is quite fitting, considering that this text is aimed at describing the process of how the little girl becomes a woman and not defining what a woman *is*. At this stage of the text, Freud names and praises three female clinicians for their outstanding contribution to the topic in hand. These analysts have already been mentioned by Freud in

"Female sexuality" (1931b). The case described in a paper titled "The analysis of a case of paranoia" (1929) by Dr Ruth Mack Brunswick, an American psychiatrist, is of great significance here. Freud believes that this was the first reported case where we see a description of a neurosis that goes back to a fixation of the pre-oedipal stage and the subject "never reached the Oedipus situation at all" (Freud, 1933a, p. 130).

In Chapter Three, this question did arise and, as evident in Brunswick's case, we now learn that it *is* possible that a little girl does *not* enter the Oedipus complex at all. Needless to say, it would not be a case without severe difficulties, extreme suffering, and a great deal of complex psychopathologies involved. Such was the case described by Brunswick, where her patient was diagnosed with paranoia with delusional jealousy, admitted to a psychiatric unit after she had suffered for a long time from violent jealousy, was arrested, and subsequently attempted to commit suicide in the police station. This case of jealous paranoia responded to analysis conducted by Brunswick. It is Brunswick's work that supports Freud's proposition that, in the pre-oedipal attachment of the little girl to her mother, one can find the germ of later paranoia (Freud, 1933a, p. 120).

Dutch psychiatrist Dr Jeanne Lampl-de Groot's work was also applauded by Freud. Her work titled "The evolution of the Oedipus complex in women" (1927) beautifully captured Freud's work unfolding in her patients. Lampl-de Groot described how, in her clinical work, she observed the significance of the little girl's pre-oedipal attachment to her mother (i.e., her phallic activity aimed at her mother). Similar to Freud, Lampl-de Groot assumed from her clinical observation that underneath the woman's positive Oedipus attitude, analysis reveals a hidden negative Oedipus attitude where the love object is the mother. Since this is revealed in the analysis later, Lampl-de Groot considered it as an attitude belonging to the pre-oedipal stage, which is in line with Freud's proposition.

Lampl-de Groot outlined two cases where laborious analytic work revealed at a later stage of analysis that the little girl's phallic activity was, indeed, aimed at the mother at the pre-oedipal stage. She also noted that the homosexual tendencies displayed by her patients in analysis seemed to be indicators of disappointments experienced by the little girl in relation to her father. This is again perfectly aligned with Freud's proposal related to the development of the masculinity complex and its relation to the disappointments received from the father (Freud, 1933a, p. 130). According to Lampl-de Groot, one of the major difficulties in accessing material from the pre-oedipal stage is establishing and maintaining transference. This is something that Freud agreed with and, hence, he relied for the most part on female analysts when it came to gaining valuable insight on female psycho-sexual development. Similar to Freud, Lampl-de Groot explains that it is difficult for a patient to go into rivalry with a male analyst in the analysis, whereas with a female analyst, the transference can be established at a much stronger level (Lampl-de Groot, 1927, p. 345).

Last, Helene Deutsch's work was also commended by Freud for her contribution. Deutsch, in her *The Psychology of Women* (1944[1932]) illustrates, as Freud recalls it, "erotic actions of homosexual women reproduce the relations between mother and baby" (Freud, 1933a, p. 131).

Further on in the text, we see Freud acknowledge that even a detailed account of feminine development through "puberty to the period of maturity" will remain as insufficient knowledge (1933a, p. 131). Hence, Freud decides to add to this discussion by emphasising a few further points. The development of femininity "remains exposed to disturbances" throughout a woman's early adult life and mature age (1933a, p. 131). These "disturbances" that Freud is referring to are the residue of the early masculine position of the girl. This might explain the frequent occurrence of women's "regression to the fixations of the pre-Oedipal phase" (1933a, p. 131). As a manifestation of such regression, some women, in the course of their lives, will be seen oscillating frequently between the periods dominated by their masculinity and femininity. What men consider as the "enigma of women" may be understood as a phenomenon occurring due to this oscillation (1933a, p. 131). Can we consider such oscillation as an "expression of bisexuality in women's lives" (1933a, p. 131)? It is Freud who poses this question and, immediately after using the term "bisexuality", Freud draws our attention to a topic that is fundamental to psychoanalytic theories: the libido and its sex.

Feminine libido

What is the motive force of human sexual life? For Freud, it is the libido. If human sexual life has two poles of masculinity and femininity, then can we consider libido as being similarly polarised as our sexual life? Can we theorise that masculine sexuality is motivated by masculine libido and, similarly, feminine sexuality by feminine libido? Freud clearly urges his readers to distance themselves from such a conclusion: "there is only one libido, which serves both the masculine and the feminine sexual function" and says that libido cannot be assigned any one sex (Freud, 1933a, p. 131). If one is inclined to equate masculine libido with activity, using the conventional methods of identifying it, then how is one to explain the existence of those trends with a passive aim that are also masculine? Therefore, Freud concludes that the expression "feminine libido" has no justification (1933a, p. 131).

Freud further asserts that he believes that when a libido "is pressed into the service of feminine function", it is applied with a lot more "constraint", meaning nature overlooks more of the feminine function's demands "than in the case of masculinity" (1933a, p. 131). In other words, Freud is proposing that, since the libido assigned to serve the feminine function is already under a lot of restraint to begin with, nature lets slide a lot of demands on the feminine function compared to that of masculinity. Freud points out one possible explanation for why nature might be taking more "careful account" of the demands made by masculine function than the feminine one. Freud speculates that, for the purpose of reproduction, considering this *is* the aim of "biology", which is a *natural* science, nature allocated aggressiveness to men and, hence, "the accomplishment of the aim of biology . . . has been made to some extent independent of women's consent" (Freud 1933a, p. 131). From this Freudian explanation, it is evident that women are in a disadvantageous position with regard to the fulfilment of biological aim. Possibly, this is why nature has compensated for its oversight by discounting a lot of the feminine function's demands. Similarly, we can extend this Freudian explanation and propose the following.

Human civilisation generated mythologies that led to the establishment of taboos (for example, incest) and social restrictions (the creation of law, ethics, rights, etc.) on the expression of masculinity in order to compensate for nature's injustice and protect women's sexual interest to some extent. This is in line with Freud's explanation that men are already assigned a monstrous amount of aggressiveness by nature which aids "the accomplishment of the aim of biology" and is, to some extent, "independent of women's consent" (1933a, p. 131).

We would not be entirely wrong in assuming and extending Freud's proposal in this manner, as the origin of the Oedipus complex, within the Freudian context, does indicate its roots in mythology (see Chapter One). Moreover, the concept of nature and nurture can be considered as "complemental" in Freud's theories, which is evident in the aetiology of neurosis, as discussed above. This interrelation between nature and nurture is also revisited extensively by Freud in *Civilisation and its Discontents* (1930a). However, we must not lose sight of the fact that psychoanalysis has not been partial or biased in the distribution of aggressiveness as an attribute between the sexes. Hence, just because "nature take less careful account of" the feminine functions demands compared to masculinity, libido that serves the feminine functions must not be considered to have less potential to cause catastrophe. The aggressive expression of the libido assigned to serve feminine functions is quite unusual and, hence, it is probably not as obvious as in libido assigned to serve the masculine function. From our reading so far, it can be proposed that such expression is to be looked for in terms of the woman's masochistic wishes within the context of the mother–child relation, her choice of object, such as partner, profession, and within other unconventional areas of her life.

Frigidity

How do we explain the phenomena of sexual frigidity, asks Freud next, acknowledging that it is a topic that has remained insufficiently understood (1933a, p. 132). In Chapter Three of this book, we have already discussed that which element or factor contributes to the sexual excitation of a woman has remained "insufficiently understood". Such is the case even in 2017, despite the significant advancements made in the field of modern medicine and science. Freud believes that, sometimes, frigidity has psychological difficulty ("psychogenic") as its aetiology (1933a, p. 132). In those cases, analysis can access the material and bring about a change but, in other cases, Freud assumes that the occurrence of frigidity is "constitutionally determined", and that there might also be an accompanying "anatomical factor" (1933a, p. 132). These comments are perfectly aligned with the current understanding of frigidity almost a century later.

Can we consider "frigidity" as the following: a person's lack of interest in sex, reduced thoughts related to sex, decrease in initiating sex, increased rejection of sexual activity, being unaffected by exposure to erotic stimuli, and decreased genital sensation during sex? These are the general criteria outlined by *DSM-5* (American Psychiatric Association, 2013) for female sexual interest/arousal disorder. The presence of any three of these symptoms during the past six months, causing significant distress in the person, will satisfy the diagnosis of this disorder. Provided, of course, that the sexual dysfunction is *not* better explained by any other mental disorder or the symptoms are *not* manifested as a consequence of other stressors, such as "severe relationship distress (e.g. partner violence)" or induced by any other medication or substance or other medical condition (American Psychiatric Association, 2013, p. 433). The *DSM-5* has merged two sexual dysfunctions, female hypoactive desire disorder and female arousal disorder, from the previous versions of the *DSM* into one. A separate disorder still exists in the *DSM-5*, called female orgasmic disorder. In short, all of these disorders can be considered as what Freud meant by the term frigidity in 1933. In terms of aetiology, it is still considered as mostly treated with psychotherapy, as the aetiology is considered as mainly psychological difficulties. Anatomical factors, too, such as medical conditions, surgery, pain during penetration, lack of lubrication, tensing of vaginal muscles, etc., *do* play a role. This is also in line with Freud's assumption in 1933. However, there is a significant difference in time with regard to one factor, which Freud called the "constitutional factor" (1933a, p. 132).

This is a factor, as we have learnt from the current text, that refers to the combined various dispositions acquired by the subject from her early infantile experience and prehistoric experience. Moreover, we cannot accept the constitutional factor as the only influencing factor in the development of a neurosis because, in cases of regression to an early infantile state, the distinct mechanism is unclear. The hesitance involved in pinning down aetiology to one distinct factor and outlining clear descriptions of the mechanisms involved in the development of neurosis are perfectly understandable, as the field of the mind is not biology. Even within the discipline of biology, we have illustrated above that answers might not always be as certain as natural or human sciences are expected to provide. Hesitation and uncertainty in the process of determining aetiology are, then, two very necessary and admirable attributes within the context of psychoanalysis because the formation of our mental life is bound to be bizzare, confusing, contradictory, and is never what it *seems* to be. Treading with caution, leaving the questions open and investigating further is necessary to treat any psychoneurosis within the context of psychoanalysis. The American Psychiatric Association (APA), however, has found two terms that are aimed at eliminating such hesitation in their process of diagnosing: "acquired" and "life-long". If the condition is not something that a person remembers to have been suffering from since he became sexually active, then it is a "life-long" condition. If there ever was a "normal sexual function", and the disturbances began after such a period, then it is "acquired". From a psychoanalytic perspective, the use of these terms in this fashion is problematic on several levels, which remain outside the scope of this book. However, there are three points that must be highlighted before continuing with our current text in hand.

1. If these two terms are to be considered as tools that help clinicians to determine whether it is a "constitutional factor" (both in the Freudian sense and as "disposition" in the ordinary sense) or not, then they are hardly serving the purpose.

2. "Becoming sexually active" is a term that is very broad and it does risk omitting valuable information about the patient's history. Within the context of psychoanalysis, this phrase is, to some extent, irrelevant and particularly poses a few questions in the light of the theories of infantile sexuality.

3. Considering a set of symptoms as a sign corresponding to a disorder raises more questions in terms of validity and reliability. For further details on the *DSM*'s reliability and validity issues related to other disorders, see *Diagnosis and the DSM: A Critical Review* (Vanheule, 2014). There is, however, a further term that explains "life-long" lack of sexual desire in today's world and it is *not* frigidity. If people self-identify as "asexual" and such self-identification better explains their lifelong lack of sexual desire, then the APA does not consider it as a disorder (American Psychiatric Association, 2014, p. 434).

Of course, a society where sexual orientation is not a disorder is evidence of progress. However, sexual orientations are now being considered as identity. Several questions arise in that case. Has the need to leave questions about one's subjective position open been superseded with the introduction of the term "asexuality"? Is there even room for a question such as this? Have we progressed since the introduction of Freud's investigation into human sexuality? These are questions that are essential to reflect upon if we are to investigate the development of human sexuality based on the markers of the drive theory.

Psychical peculiarity of mature femininity

"We do not lay claim to more than an average validity for these assertions; nor is it always easy to distinguish what should be ascribed to the influence of the sexual function and what to social breeding" (Freud, 1933a, p. 132)

This comment captures Freud's position towards the end of his lecture. Continuing with the text, we see Freud providing us with more examples of "psychical peculiarity of mature femininity" drawing from clinical observation (Freud, 1933a, p. 132). As the comment above suggests, there is always a difficulty in determining how much of her internal experience and how much of her external factors influence the little girl's psychosexual development. However, it is important to examine all the possible factors and influences contributing to the construction of femininity. Narcissism is one of those primary factors and *this* particular factor influences women's choice of object.

Narcissistic object-choice

Narcissism is an essential psychical mechanism for the child's development; it is one of the fundamental theories in psychoanalysis and, at the same time, it is an extremely complex concept to comprehend. Very briefly, the term narcissism is a reference to the myth of Narcissus, where love is directed to one's image of oneself (Laplanche & Pontalis, 1973, p. 255). To put the concept of narcissism within the context of sexual disposition, it will be useful to highlight the following. In *Psycho-analytic Notes on an Autobiographical Account of a Case of Paranoia*, otherwise known as the Schreber case, Freud wrote,

> In my *Three Essays on the Theory of Sexuality* I have expressed the opinion that each stage in the development of psychosexuality affords

a possibility of "fixation" and thus a dispositional point. People who have not freed themselves completely from the stage of narcissism . . . have at that point a fixation which may operate as a disposition to later illness. (Freud, 1911c, p. 62)

To put it in the perspective of libido, one can succinctly describe narcissism as follows. Freud considered the ego as a reservoir of libido. Considering that a clear-cut distinction such as the following does not do justice to Freud's theory, it can be said that, when libido takes one's own ego as an object, it can be regarded as ego-libido, and when libido is directed towards an object apart from one's own ego, it can be regarded as object-libido. In "On narcissism", Freud described that the more one of these increases, the more the other decreases and this "antithesis between ego-libido and object-libido" is a fundamental concept of human relations within the context of psychoanalysis (Freud, 1914c, p. 76). To repeat, this is an extremely difficult distinction to make and it is not to be understood as a clear marker. Only in the analysis of severe neurosis and psychosis are these processes revealed as identifiable (Freud, 1914c, p. 77). Freud further explains that human beings choose their objects and direct their libido on to it, based on their fixations and dispositions. He proposes that there are two kinds of object choice available to all human beings—anaclitic object choice and narcissistic object choice (Freud, 1914c, p. 88).

According to Freud, a prime characteristic of most men would be anaclitic object choice, where the object is sexually over-valued due to the transference of the subject's original narcissism to the sexual object (Freud, 1914c, p .88), whereas most women, especially if they are bestowed with "good-looks" and have developed a sense of "self-contentment", will make narcissistic object choice (Freud, 1914c, p. 89). It is almost as if women who make a narcissistic object choice perceive their physical attributes and charm as a "compensation" for the "social restriction" they have been subjected to (914c, p. 89). This kind of object choice involves the subjects *loving themselves* more than they are *being loved* by the other, and the emphasis lies *not* in "the direction of loving, but of being loved" (Freud, 1914c, p. 89). It can be questioned whether a narcissistic object choice is a reproduction of the child's original relationship to his or her mother (Laplanche & Pontalis, 1973, p. 259). The similarities are striking because, during the early years of the child's life, the child *receives* love, food, care, warmth, and affection and does not concern himself with returning the favour. Similarly, narcissistic object choice is more concerned with being loved than loving. It is worth repeating here that Freud agrees that both men and women are capable of making either object choice and that is evident even in the clinics of today.

Returning to the text, we see Freud referring to the above theory and stating that some women make a narcissistic object choice because "to be loved is a stronger need for them than to love" (Freud, 1933a, p. 132). But now Freud adds to this theory and suggests that it is penis envy that is essential in understanding women's narcissistic object choice. The realisation that they lack a penis, which mortifies them, leads women to "value their charms more highly as a late compensation for the original sexual inferiority" (Freud, 1933a, p. 132). Now, we can question if a man is making narcissistic object choice, then are they "valuing their charms more" as a compensation for some kind of "inferiority"? Is this inferiority still referring to a lack of a penis in men, or some other restriction they have felt they have been subjected to? Or is this inferiority arising from the fear of being castrated? Is castration, then, only referring to the lack of a penis or restrictions and limits of a different kind? Is the term femininity referring to only a woman who is biologically a female, or would it be wiser to consider femininity as a "feminine position"? As we will see in the next chapter, Lacan's investigation into human psychosexual development follows a similar line of argument. For now, we agree that castration is a Freudian concept that refers to the realisation of a little girl of the lack of a penis in both herself and women in general, and penis envy is the envy developed in women due to this lack.

Shame

Freud then proceeds to highlight the characteristics of shame, which is so often attributed to the nature of femininity. Considering that the text was written in 1933 in German, the term "shame" might also be referring to the expression of emotions such as shy and introverted. The frequency with which one notices such characteristics in women in today's modern world is not the same as it was around the early 1900s. Drawing from modern clinical encounters in today's world, it can be added that the same characteristics are also frequently seen in little boys and in young and adult men. This raises several questions when considering the explanation Freud provides for the characteristic of shame in women. Freud believes that shame is not just a "matter of convention"; rather, it emerges from the idea of "concealment of genital deficiency" (Freud, 1933a, p. 132). He acknowledges that shame "takes on other functions" in a woman's life and he explains his position by highlighting a particular discovery and invention made by women—"plaiting and weaving" (1933a, p. 132). Freud speculates that the unconscious motive behind this invention can be connected to an inspiration of the model invented by mother nature. In other words, Freud proposes that women's invention of plaiting and weaving is an imitation of a model provided by nature. In women's bodies the manner of growth of the "pubic hair" causes it to become "matted together" and, thus, a natural weaving occurs which "conceals the genitals" (Freud, 1933a, p. 132). Freud agrees that if such a connection seems far-fetched and if we regard his belief "in the influence of lack of a penis on the configuration of femininity as an *idée fixe*", then he is, of course, "defenceless" (Freud, 1933a, p. 132). How do we make sense of such an interpretation? If it provokes something within us, then what is it provoking and why are we feeling such reactions? On the other hand, if we agree with this interpretation, then what does that indicate about our own perception of femininity? It is essential that we enquire within us and question our rationalisations and emotions while reading Freud. After all, it *is* psycho*analysis* that we are venturing into and unless we analyse ourselves, a lot of what we are reading will remain at a level of knowledge *studied* but not *acquired*.

Ambivalence

Freud believes that the factors that influence the woman's choice of object often become unrecognisable due to social conditions (1933a, p. 132). In other words, during the early 1900s, at the time of the drafting of these theories, society was a very different place for women than it is now. A woman's choice of clothing, hobbies, friends, career, husband—almost everything was predetermined, limited, or, in a sense, restricted. Under such conditions, it was difficult to differentiate between the choices that were made by a woman due to her own libidinal investment and those that were chosen *for* her by society. Freud also thinks that often the girl would make choices that are in line with the "narcissistic ideal of the man whom the girl had wished to become" (Freud, 1933a, pp. 132–133). If the girl remains in her Oedipus complex, then her attachment to her father will influence her choice of object and they might be in accordance with the "parental type" (Freud, 1933a, p. 133).

To begin with, the girl had an ambivalent relationship with her mother. Hence, when she turned from her mother towards her father, the element of hostility in her ambivalent relationship to her mother should restrict itself only to the mother and "should guarantee a happy marriage" (Freud, 1933a, p. 133). But often this is not the case. The settlement of the conflict due to her ambivalence will always pose a threat to her future relationship with her partner (1933a, p. 133). The element of hostility that we thought she left behind when she turned away from her mother does not remain inactive. Rather, it can find its way to a new object, her partner. The girl might transfer to her husband the feeling of hostility that originally was aimed at her mother. Hence, very often, the second half of the woman's life is spent struggling against her husband in the very same way that she spent the first half of her life struggling against her mother (Freud, 1933a, p. 133). Freud suggests that often a second marriage seems much more satisfying due to the fact that the girl has already gone through and exhausted her hostility on her first choice of object (after mother and father), which, in this case, would be her first husband (Freud, 1933a, p. 133).

In "The taboo of virginity", Freud highlighted another possible reason for the woman's transference of her hostility against her mother to her first husband: "a woman's *immature sexuality* is discharged on to the man who first makes her acquainted with the sexual act" (1918a, p. 206). Let us consider the following. The mother, who was responsible for the little girl's mundane hygiene routine, was perceived by the girl as her first seducer. The mother was perceived as someone whose activities led the little girl to first discover sexual excitation. Such excitation and activities were later discouraged by the same mother who introduced them to her in the first place. Now, considering that she is a virgin, which is evident in Freud's text, the transference of the hostility to the woman's husband seems quite possible, since she is once again faced with another seducer. The fear of her relation with her husband ending in a betrayal, as it did with her mother, might, quite possibly, be an unconscious influence which reproduces the previously felt hostility in the woman.

The baby

After the first child is born, the couple's life goes through various difficulties. Freud suggests that when a woman becomes a mother herself,
the identification with her own mother and the feelings of hostility
and ambivalence that she has been long struggling with are once
again revived (Freud, 1933a, p. 133). For a detailed discussion of the
effect of motherhood in relation to the woman's pre-oedipal attachment and hostility towards her mother, see Chapter Three. However,
Freud adds something new to this topic in this text from 1933. Here,
Freud outlines one particular perspective very clearly. Becoming a
mother herself does not only influence the transference of the
woman's previous feelings towards her mother, but "the compulsion
to repeat reproduces an unhappy marriage between her parents"
(Freud, 1933a, p. 133). This is a much more complex proposal than any
of his previous writings on the topic of becoming a mother. It is often
believed that becoming parents is one of the most joyous, and yet one
of the most chaotic, times of a couple's life. Mostly, the difficulties
inherent to this time are explained by the new arrival's excessive
demands and the disruption it causes to the couple's usual routine.
The relationship between the couple is often expected to go through a
certain amount of turmoil after the birth of the first child, as, obviously, the dynamics of the nuclear family changes completely. The
story of two suddenly becomes the story of three. The mother herself
has once been where her child is now. It is quite possible that the
memories of herself being a child are now revived. It is also possible
that such memories will now influence her to reshape the dynamics
between her and her husband, just like what she remembers happen-
ing between her parents. What other ways can we explain Freud's
proposal that the revival of the mother's infantile experience influences the reproduction of her parents' unhappy marriage after the
birth of her first child?

Freud also observes that there is a difference between the mother's
reaction to the birth of a son and to that of a daughter. Freud attributes this difference in the mother's reaction to the influence of penis
envy in the mother, which he believes "has not lost its strength"
(Freud, 1933a, p. 133). It is, of course, understandable that, during the
early 1900s, a boy's life would be much more unrestricted in many
senses than a girl's life and, hence, a mother might prefer to have boy

in order to save him from the difficulties and miseries that she experienced while growing up herself simply for being a girl. But can we overlook the power she would have gained in such a society for simply delivering a boy child? Can we overlook the immediate boost in her social status, both in the wider society and in her own family, for delivering a boy child? Can we overlook the fact that we still live in a patriarchal society, where a child usually takes their father's surname and, thus, only a boy is paramount in society's perception of maintaining the ancestral line and the family name? Could these be the factors that explain the mother's preference for a boy child? How do we explain the difference in the mother's reaction to having a boy child in the *modern world* to that when she has a little girl? In many parts of the world currently, there are still efforts being made to make it illegal to determine the sex of the foetus due to the fear of female infanticide. It is needless to mention that gender discrimination still exists in various forms and degrees across the world.

Do these societal connotations attached to gender have any influence in the formation of penis envy in the little girl's psyche from the moment she discovers she is castrated? If one is to embark on a psychoanalytic exploration of human sexuality, then societal influence in the development of penis envy should not be prioritised over the examination of the subjective reality and the working of the mental life of that particular individual. This is precisely because internal reality and the influence it has on our psychical mechanisms are independent of factual or external reality.

Freud further highlights that a mother and son relationship is "the most perfect, the most free from ambivalence of all human relationships" (1933a, p. 133). Why is that the case? How are the other human relationships not so "perfect" or not so "free from ambivalence"? In *Group Psychology and the Analysis of the Ego* (1921c), Freud asserted that almost all "intimate human relation between two people which lasts for some time", such as marriage, friendship, parental relation contain an element of "aversion and hostility", which might not be remembered at times due to the work of repression (Freud, 1921c, p. 100). However, there is only one exception to this proposal, which is the mother and son relationship, and it is possibly due to the following reasons. This is a bond based on narcissism, there is no "subsequent rivalry", and it is "reinforced by rudimentary attempt at sexual-object" (Freud, 1921c, p. 101, n). The mother seems to find in her son the compensation for the injustice she has been subjected to. For Freud, the mother and son relationship is the purest example of a human bond where affection remains unchangeable, and "unimpaired by any egoistic consideration" (Freud, 1916–1917, p. 206). Freud returns to the subject again in *Civilization and its Discontents* (1930a), and states that aggressiveness is the foundation of "every relation of affection and love among people" except in the case of the mother's relation to her male child (1930a, p. 113). This narcissistic bond with her son provides "unlimited satisfaction" to the mother (1933a, p. 133). In Chapter Six, we discuss how troubling this might be for the girl child who is aware that the boy is the source of "unlimited satisfaction" for her mother, according to Lacan. What purpose does the son serve for the mother that the little boy can satisfy her so profoundly? Freud further explains how a son might be the answer to all that the mother has been looking for. He notes that all the ambition that the mother has had to suppress within her she can now transfer to her son; she can also expect her son to appease all that she renounced and all that is left behind of her masculinity complex (Freud, 1933a, p. 133). Motherly love also secures a marriage if the wife succeeds "in making her husband her child" and "acting as a mother to him" (Freud, 1933a, p. 133). In the light of these postulations, are we beginning to see the insatiable need in human beings to be loved unconditionally, the need to recreate the time of our early years where the primary concern was to be loved and taken care of, but not have to return the favour? Does that not indicate that, at a fundamental level, all human beings are equipped with the ability to make narcissistic object-choices, to use Freudian terminology, and that probably we *are* all making them everyday at some level?

A woman's love

There are two distinct levels in the identification of a woman with her mother (Freud, 1933a, p. 134): (1) the girl's "affectionate attachment" to her mother during her pre-oedipal phase, where she wishes to walk in her footsteps and idealises her, and (2) in the Oedipus complex, where she wishes to get rid of her mother and take the mother's place with her father. Freud believes that both phases remain somewhat unnegotiated in the path of her future development. A lot of it remains unresolved and its effect seeps into her future. Freud stresses the idea that the pre-Oedipus attachment of the little girl is a decisive factor for her future. All the future characteristics that she is about to acquire, her individuality, her peculiarity, all that she would use to "later fulfil her role in the sexual function and perform her invaluable social tasks", the preparation for all of that takes place during her pre-oedipal phase (Freud, 1933a, p. 134). It is this pre-oedipal phase, in her identification with her mother, that the little girl "acquires her attractiveness to a man" (1933a, p. 134). The man, on the other hand, owing to *his* Oedipus attachment to *his* mother, feels passionate about the girl when he falls for her attractiveness (1933a, p. 134). Then again, it would be this man's son who "obtains" in future "what he himself aspired to" (p. 134). The one he "aspired to" is his wife, but, unfortunately, no human relation is freed from aggressiveness and "egoistic consideration", including that of the mother to her son. This is why Freud concluded that it seems to be "that a man's love and woman's are a phase apart psychologically" (Freud, 1933a, p. 134).

Sense of justice and envy

Are women regarded as "having little sense of justice" (Freud, 1933a, p. 134)? It is not clear in Freud's comment as to whose perception this is. If this is a general perception, then what are the particular characteristics of women that are influencing such a perception? A similar notion had already been discussed by Freud in theorising women's formation of the superego: their sense of right and wrong. Earlier, Freud illustrated how, due to the fact that women do not have a penis, there is an obvious threat missing in the case of women and the rigidity of the formation of their superegos cannot be compared to that of men's. This means the influencing factors in the formation of the superego are much more robust and active in the case of men, due to the threat of castration. At this stage in the text, Freud again revisits this topic of women's sense of justice, but this time he connects it to the "predominance of envy in their mental life" (Freud, 1933a, p. 134). He justifies this connection in the following way: "the demand for justice is a modification of envy and lays down the condition subject to which one can put envy aside" (Freud, 1933a, p. 134). It becomes a bit clearer from this comment that, by "little sense of justice", Freud is alluding to the notion that women's demands for justice might be extreme or disproportionate and that perhaps, at times, it seems that women have a harsh sense of justice. He interprets this characteristic as the following. The call for justice is arising from envy, as justice sets aside what is fair and what is not and, thus, envy can still operate in relation to what has been set aside as unjust. This is a unique interpretation of penis envy and its relation to women's sense of justice, which Freud did not outline in his previous texts examined in this book. In the light of this view, we can pose the following question. If similar characteristics of "little sense of justice" are displayed by a man, do we overlook the connection between such characteristics and the man's sense of envy, simply because he is *not without* a penis? Or, in that case, can we not theorise that envy is a significant factor, which develops out of a lack, and it can lead to the impairment of one's sense of justice? But we must remind ourselves that such a hypothesis would be based on a lack that does not restrict itself to the organ, the penis. Within the Freudian context, it is, however, very clear that Freud refers to the lack of the *penis* in relation to the theories of castration and penis envy.

Love is for two

The next interpretation Freud makes is much more difficult to understand. He claims that women are "weaker in their social interests" and that women tend to have "less capacity for sublimating their instincts than men" (Freud, 1933a, p. 134). Consider the first part of the quotation concerning women's social interests. This might seem intelligible if we refer to his earlier work, illustrated in *Group Psychology and the Analysis of the Ego* (1921c). For the formation and sustainment of a group, it is essential that the "characters of instincts" are "inhibited in their aims" (Freud, 1921c, p. 140). When a sexual aim is unattainable due to internal or external obstacles, they are referred to as sexual impulsions that are inhibited in their aims (1921c, p. 140). While the expression of such instincts that are inhibited in their aims might seem socially acceptable, one must not lose sight of the notion that such instincts arise directly out of sexual instincts. This would suggest that the formation of a group might be threatened if direct sexual instincts are not inhibited in their aims.

In the history of the development of the family, to begin with there were group relations such as group sexual activities, the herd approach to sexuality, group love, group marriages, one or more men for many women, and *vice versa*, etc. With the development of civili-sation and sophistication, sexual love became more important for the ego. Such changes influenced the development of "the characteristics of being in love" over time, and, along with this, the requirement to limit sexual love to only two people became urgent, which is also in line with what is "prescribed by the nature of the genital aim" (Freud, 1921c, p. 140). Polygamous inclinations were restricted to satisfying themselves only by a change of objects (Freud, 1921c, p. 140). Freud, thus, considered that when two people seek solitude in each other and unite for sexual satisfaction, they are acting "against the herd instinct, the group feeling" (1921c. p. 140). This intention of encroachment on, and protection of, the choice of sexual object is in direct opposition to the mentality of the group. The expression of love in the form that involves two people is, thus, an expression of the rejection of group instincts and, as such, is often expressed in the feeling of shame (Freud, 1921c, p. 140). The feeling of jealousy is also expressed when the choice of sexual object seems in/exclusive and this could lead to violence, which is evident in the history of crimes committed under the influence of passion (1921c, p. 140).

Since, according to Freud, most women would choose to make narcissistic object choices, it can be proposed that exclusivity of the sexual object becomes crucial for the sustainment of the ego. This is precisely what is against the group instinct and this is possibly what Freud means by the comment that women are "weaker in their social interests" (Freud, 1933a, p. 134). This is also evident in his further explanation that such a reduced social interest of women is also a characteristic of all sexual relations in general (1933a, p. 134). The feel-ing of being in love provides a sense of "sufficiency in each other" and, similarly, a family unit, too, displays expressions of protective-ness and might resist the inclusion of other associations (1933a, p. 134). This would suggest that it is not just women, but men, too, who are capable of being "weaker in social interests", but the theory of penis envy does not apply to them. What loss would motivate their feelings of envy, jealousy, and shame? Do all humans suffer from an inherent lack? The Freudian theory of castration would suggest so. If it is not a loss of the penis, it might be the fear of losing the penis.

According to Lacanian theories, this would correlate with the lack within all of us, the presence of which is essential for the emergence and activation of desire, something that is absent in depression and melancholia. We can also pose other questions in this connection, as follows. The need for individual ego satisfaction influenced the emergence of the need to restrict sexual love to two people during the course of human civilisation. If that has been the case, then, in our current society, where individual satisfaction is favoured over collective satisfaction, what is the future of love? What would be our future expressions of our directly sexual impulses and where would they be taking us? Would there be a further tightening of the restrictions in the already encroached couple relation, or would there be an opposite effect and a possible return to the interests of the group instincts? At the same time, it would be useful to keep in mind that, even in the primal herd, there have been reasons for marking the woman as "taken" by the man for the purposes of recognising their own children and providing protection for the children. For example, Indian married women wear *bindi* and *sindoor*, bangles and anklets to symbolise that they are "taken", or married, which is in line with the ancient rituals of hitting women on the head with a rock, making them bleed, and putting shackles around their wrists and ankles. Such acts were performed men to mark their "territory". It is unclear whether such acts were performed out of love for the woman, or for their future children, or for the purposes of boosting their own social status among the herd. However, they *did* involve the satisfaction of sexual love and, thus, the possible satisfaction of the ego is hardly unnoticeable in these instances. Although these tales of such "marking" of women have almost disappeared from the colloquial stories, the rituals have now become a fashion statement for most women in India.

With regard to Freud's comment about women having ". . . less capacity for sublimating their instincts than men" (1933a, p. 134), it must be mentioned to begin with that sublimation is a process that Freud referred to throughout his career. Acknowledging the density and complexity of this process, only a brief account of this term is provided here for the purpose of our discussion in hand. Sublimation is a process that can refer to human activities which do not seem to have any "apparent connection with sexuality but which are assumed to be motivated by the force of the sexual instinct" (Laplanche & Pontalis, 1973, p. 431). Freud's position in relation to the process of sublimation in 1933 was as follows. In Lecture XXXII, "Anxiety and instinctual life", Freud explained that "a certain kind of modification of the aim and change of the object, in which our social valuation is taken into account, is described by us as 'sublimation'" (Freud, 1933a, p. 97). "Artistic creation and intellectual enquiry" are the two main types of activities that Freud described in relation to the process of sublimation (Laplanche & Pontalis, 1973, p. 431). Is it possible that Freud was inclined to draw such a conclusion regarding women's ability to sublimate based on his time and experience? Can we justify his comment by considering that the two activities specified were not often performed by women in the late 1800s and the early 1900s, mainly due to the social restrictions women were subjected to, which differed afterwards? This might be the case, as Freud himself contradicts his comment in the same text and notes that "the aptitude for sublimation is subject to the greatest individual variation" (Freud 1933a, p. 134), which means every individual will vary in his or her ability and capacity to sublimate. However, are we to consider the inclusion of this comment as a *correction*?

The next lines would suggest otherwise. Freud's earlier comment about women's lesser ability to sublimate is, indeed, based on his clinical observations. He is perplexed by the observation that a man of an average age of thirty displays more flexibility, youthfulness, and more openness to the possibilities of further development revealed to him in the process of analysis than a woman of the same age (Freud, 1933a, p. 134). Freud highlights that a thirty-year-old woman would often "frighten" the clinicians with her "psychical rigidity and unchangeability" (Freud, 1933a, p. 135). It seems to Freud that, in the case of a woman, her libido has chosen a final position, and it "seems incapable of exchanging them for others" (1933a, p. 135). It seems as if the woman does not want to recognise any possibility of further development; "the whole process has already run its course" and, hence, her libido is "insusceptible to influence" (1933a, p. 135). Freud explains that such rigidity might be due to the complexity of the development of her psychosexuality that she has already experienced. It is evident from this text that this might be the case, that the development of femininity has been an exhausting process for her and that it has already negated all further possibilities of development (Freud, 1933a, p. 135). Hence, Freud concludes that the question of femininity remains as a "lament" for clinicians, even in cases where analytic work manages to put an end to the "patient's ailment by doing away with her neurotic conflict" (1933a, p. 135).

Along with Freud, it must be acknowledged that his account of femininity in this text has been "certainly incomplete", "fragmentary", and, at times, it might even have seemed not very "friendly" (Freud, 1933a, p. 135). Yet, the description he provides of women in this text refers only to their "sexual function" (1933a, p. 135). Freud emphasises that, although a woman's sexual functions do influence a lot more than just her sexuality, certainly one should not overlook that an individual woman also serves several other functions, due to the very fact that she is a human being. Hence, for further knowledge on the subject of femininity, Freud encourages his readers to learn from their own life experiences, or look for the answers in poetry or literature. Otherwise, we could wait for science to provide us with a "deeper and more coherent" (1933a, p. 135) understanding of femininity. However, that does not seem to be the case, even after almost a century has passed since Freud's investigation into feminine sexuality.

To sum up, Freud redeveloped and repeated several of his previous theories on the castration complex and its effect on the development of feminine psychosexuality. In Freud's interpretation, it has been evident that the line of development that Freud posited as the "normal" path to femininity is not without its own difficulties and complexities. Moreover, questions still remain open on the development of a little girl's superego and how it deals with her inherent feeling of loss, which, for Freud, is the loss of the penis.

The next chapter examines how Jacques Lacan conceptualises castration in his Seminar IV, where one of the central themes is the Little Hans case.

CHAPTER SIX

Castration for Lacan: Seminar IV (1956–1957)

Introduction

In this chapter, we will examine Lacan's reformulation of the castration complex by focusing on two lectures from Seminar IV: "The structure of myths in the observation of the phobia of Little Hans – on the Oedipus complex" (1957, pp. 226–245) and "On the castration complex" (1957, pp. 246–265). The aim is to highlight Lacan's perspectives on the Freudian theories of castration and link them to the findings of the previous chapters. It is the case of Little Hans (Freud, 1909b) that embodies Freud's first discussion on the concept of the castration complex. Hence, these two lectures by Lacan, where he uses the same case to reformulate and revise Freud's theories of the castration complex, would be an excellent starting point.

Lacan's terminologies

Lacan's expressions are distinctive in nature. Although it is beyond the scope of this chapter to explain all the relevant terminologies, the following explication of terms is aimed at situating Lacan and his line of enquiry in the mid 1950s, in as much as it is necessary for the discussion in hand. First, Lacan refers to the subject and, second, Lacan's structural model of the unconscious in the mid 1950s is aligned with the Saussurian model of language. For Lacan, "to be structured" means "to be like a language" and, hence, Lacan considered that "the unconscious is structured like a language" (Evans, 1996, p. 193). The emphasis remains on the word "like" because, for Lacan, the unconscious is *not* language, but is *like* a language. Just as language has rules and codes that must be obeyed by the speaker, the subject's relation to the Law structures him. The term "structure", thus, refers to the way the subject organises his relation to the external world within his internal world, "the internal representation of interpersonal relations" (Evans, 1996, p. 193). In other words, it is how a subject situates or positions himself or herself in relation to the "other subjects and other signifiers" (Evans, 1996, p. 193). There are three possible positions that the subject can take in relation to the Other (the term "Other" will be explained shortly) and these positions are known as the subject's structure: neurosis, perversion, and psychosis. However, a subject can only be of a neurotic or a perverse or a psychotic structure, but not a neurotic and a psychotic structure at the same time. This is because there are three distinct mechanisms involved in the constitution of these structures. For example, the mechanism for the neurotic structure is repression, for the perverse structure it is disavowal, and for psychosis it is foreclosure. To put it succinctly, repression, disavowal, and foreclosure are, thus, mechanisms involved in the organisation of the subject's structure in relation to castration. In other words, the subject can repress or disavow or foreclose castration.

Lacan also uses three orders, or registers, as a classification system to conceptualise his theories: Symbolic, Imaginary, and Real (Evans, 1996, pp. 131–132). Unlike Freud, who frequently uses the term "penis", occasionally "phallic", and rarely ""phallus", Lacan mostly uses the term "phallus" (see Chapter X for details). Lacan conceptualises the phallus in the three registers: symbolic, imaginary, and the real phallus. Phallus represents the signifier of desire. Similarly, he also conceptualises the father in the three registers and emphasises the father's *function* rather than the father's *role*. Lacan uses the term "lack" in relation to desire. In this particular seminar, he refers to lack as lack of an object and he identifies three different forms of lack:

privation, frustration, and castration. This chapter does not intend to elaborate on the first two concepts; they are explored in Chapter Seven.

It is via object lack or loss that desire comes into play. Castration, for Lacan, is a symbolic act concerning an imaginary object loss where the agent is the real father. Finally, the notion of the "other/Other" is the most complex and yet the crucial one in grasping Lacan's arguments (Evans, 1996, p. 132). Put very briefly, the "other" is situated in the imaginary order, the projection of the ego or the specular image; the "Other" belongs to the symbolic order, the realm of language and the law (Evans, 1996, p. 132). Psychoanalytic interventions aim at situating the subject in his or her subjective symbolic, because, for Lacan, the Other is the locus of the subject's desire and, hence, the analyst positions herself in the place of the capitalised Other, and the analysis thus operates at the level of the symbolic and not the imaginary, that is, ego–ego identification.

The oedipal dialectic and Hans

Unlike Freud, the mother–child relationship for Lacan is never a duality. Similar to his other foundational theories, Lacan also describes the mother–child relationship in terms of a trio. There is a third element: the phallus. I shall highlight two instances from the lectures being examined where Lacan's theorisation of the phallus is the most clear. First, the phallus is an imaginary element in the dyad relationship of the mother and the child (1957, p. 228). Lacan refers to this triangular situation (mother–child–phallus) as the pre-oedipal phase. Since, Lacan conceptualises the Oedipus complex as a dialectical process, this triangular situation changes in the Oedipus complex. In order to grasp this change in the dialectic process of the Oedipus complex, the second instance of Lacan's theorisation of phallus is useful. Lacan emphasises that at the border of the pre-oedipal stage and the Oedipus complex lies the process where the child is to assume this imaginary phallus as signifier, "in a way which makes it [the phallus] the symbolic order of exchanges, in so far as it presides over the constitution of lineages" (1957, p. 228). In other words, the child has not only to see beyond the imaginary function of the phallus, that the phallus is a signifier, but he also has to accept this signifier as a governing element in the very structure of the genealogy. Hence, at the heart of the oedipal dialectic lies the issue of the child "being confronted with that order", the order that I would call the governing role of the phallus as a signifier in the structuring of genealogy (1957, p. 228). However, there can be stagnation in this process and, when it occurs, it calls for an intervention. According to these two particular lectures, such interventions may arise (1) in the form of the subject's own production of phobia or paranoia, (2) via the real father, and/or (3) analytic intervention, which can function as a substitute for the symbolic father.

Keeping in line with the aim of this book, and acknowledging the depth of Lacan's theory on the Oedipus complex, only one crucial aspect of Lacan's theory will be highlighted below: his emphasis on the function of the father. It is in the function of the father that the governing role of the phallus as a signifier is to be grasped in Lacan's theories.

In this particular seminar, Lacan questions the normalising function of the Oedipus complex, at the end of which the subject is supposed to make an object choice and, moreover, this choice must be heterosexual; at least, such is the case according to psychoanalytic theories (1957, p. 230). Lacan noted that there are many different forms of apparent heterosexuality. In certain cases, the heterosexual relation can be traced back to a "homosexualised position" (p. 230). This is similar to what Freud wrote, ". . . in addition to their manifest heterosexuality, a very considerable measure of latent or unconscious homosexuality can be detected in all normal people" (Freud, 1920a, p. 171). This is evident in Freud's theory which stresses the notion that the finding of an object is always a "refinding" of the object lost at the beginning of the subject's formation (Freud, 1905d, p. 222). According to Freud, anaclitic and narcissistic are the two methods of finding an object, theories which have been discussed in Chapter Five. According to both Freud and Lacan, the first love object is always the mother. Hence, Lacan emphasises that the subject's object choice can be traced back to the way in which the Oedipus complex was navigated, where such choices are not a given precisely because there is no predetermined harmony between the drive and the object (Lacan, 1957, p. 59). This is again a reference to Freud's theory of the drive:

> the object [objekt] of an instinct is the thing in regard to which or
> through which the instinct is able to achieve its aim. It is what is most

variable about an instinct and is not in consequence of being pecu-
liarly fitted to make satisfaction possible. (Freud, 1915c, p. 122)

Moreover, Freud outlined that this object can be "a part of the subject's own body", the object may change several times "in the course
of the vicissitudes which the instinct undergoes during its existence",
there can be "displacement of instincts", and, if there is to be a close
attachment of the object with its aim, then it is to be understood as
"fixation" (Freud, 1915c, pp. 122–123). This comment would suggest
that there is no predetermined object for the instinct. That which satisfies the instinct will always be variable and, at times, might even seem
peculiar. However, when stagnation occurs, it is to be comprehended
as a fixation of the libido. Hence, it must be highlighted here that the
idea of *being born with a certain sexual preference* raises questions when
it is examined through the drive theory. Lacan proposes that at the
centre of the Oedipus complex lies this fundamental problem: how
the subjects (both a boy and a girl) situate themselves in relation to the
function of the father (1957, p. 233). For Lacan, the goal of the Oedipus
complex in boys is not just an identification of the subject with the
parent of his own sex, which is an *imaginary relation* to the father, but,
rather, it is about *how* the subject situates himself in terms of the *function of the father* and through which he perceives a future wherein he
will one day inherit and occupy the "problematic and paradoxical
position of being a father" (1957, p. 233).

It can be argued that Lacan added to the list of questions that
Freud highlighted in relation to infantile sexual researches (Chapter
One). The bigger question for Lacan, at this stage of his teaching, is
"'what is to be a father?'" (p. 233). Lacan sums up the Freudian investigation of the Oedipus complex in this very question. This question
is in line with Freudian articulation of infantile puzzlement regarding
the distinction between the sexes, the origin of babies (the father's role
in it), and children's creation of myth in response to such questions.
This was also evident in Little Hans' case study. The comment below
illustrates how Hans asks his father the very question Lacan highlights as the centre of the Oedipus complex: what it is to be a father.
In this innocent question of Hans, it is also apparent that it is more
than that. Hans is puzzled and he is wondering how he is to situate
himself with regard to both his father and also to the question of himself being a father.

"*I*: 'Do you know why you wish for it? It's because you'd like to be a Daddy.'" "*Hans*: 'Yes . . . How does it work?'" "*I*: 'How does what work?'" "*Hans*: 'You say Daddies don't have babies; so how does it work, my wanting to be Daddy?'" (Freud, 1909b, p. 92)

The problem is not solely posed for the child in relation to the signifier "father", or the father within the family, but also remains a question even when the subject accedes to the paternal position himself, such as the question of procreation. Lacan noted that not only is the question of the father a problem for every neurotic and non-neurotic, Freud's research, too, is orientated around this question (Lacan, 1957, pp. 233–234). (The non-neurotic's response to the question of procreation is explored in Chapter Seven.) Lacan illustrates this by describing that Freud invented the myth of the father for a significant reason. The fathers portrayed in Freud's case studies seem to be real and human (i.e., flawed), marked with their own limitations. They do not seem to fit the menacing and threatening castrating father that Freud describes in his theory of the Oedipus complex. Freud needed the father to fill the gap between his clinical observations and his theoretical formulations. This is evident in Lacan's comment, ". . . *Totem and Taboo*, [which] is nothing other than a modern myth, a myth constructed to explain what remained gaping in his doctrine, which was—*Where is the father?*" (1957, p. 241). In the dialectic of the Oedipus complex, Lacan proposes that one starts from the position of a certain assumption, which is the notion that somewhere, someone must fully guarantee the position of the father to the subject and reply, "*I am the father*" (p. 233). For Lacan, "this assumption is essential to the whole progress of the Oedipal dialectic" (p. 234). But who was this guarantor in Hans' case?

In Hans' case, at the pre-phobic phase, Lacan believes Hans was in a game of lure with his mother. By "lure", Lacan refers to his "seductive activities towards his mother" (p. 229). What is at stake in the Oedipus situation, for Lacan, is that the subject himself becomes "caught in this lure" (p. 229). In other words, in Lacan's formulation of the Oedipus complex, unlike Freud's, the subjects themselves experience an anxiety about disappearing as a subject and it is not due to the fear of the father. This anxiety is very different from Freud's formulation of castration, where the child fears the castrating father. The subject being "caught in this lure", is a fear of being reduced to nothing, being devoured, disappearing in the real. This is an anxiety that *calls for* an intervention, *not fears* an intervention. It is an anxiety that produces phobia as a solution, possibly because there was no guarantor, as such.

It is important to emphasise that, for Lacan, the father exists in the three registers: imaginary father, symbolic father, and the real father. If the whole oedipal dialect is based on the function of the father, then Lacan is referring to this interplay of the father in the three registers. How are we to conceptualise the father in these three registers? Freud emphasised that, at the entry into the Oedipus complex, there is rivalry with the father. Lacan agrees with this view, but he highlights that this aggressiveness is a fundamental imaginary conflict that intervenes: "either me or the other" (p. 236). In other words, this is a specular relation situated in the imaginary plane. This is the imaginary father, in these two lectures of Lacan. However, that does not sum up the whole oedipal situation for Lacan.

For Freud, the Oedipus complex is finally resolved when the hostility towards the father is repressed. When a resolution (destruction of the Oedipus complex) takes place in response to a crisis (the oedipal crisis), it leaves its mark in the unconscious: the superego. Lacan reinterpreted this and suggested that the oedipal relation must produce something new and original, and described this as the Other, the symbolic. Lacan suggests that, for the Oedipus complex to exist at the level of the Other, a term must be produced that would signify someone who was not involved in the game before, and this is the one who is in the position to both play and win the game (p. 238), someone who has the winning card, who knows and has the phallus, the true, real penis (p. 239).

In the case history, it is evident that Hans was not discovering the phallus anywhere. His mother said she had it, but he discovered that it was not there (the incident of Hans watching his mother undress). His sister did not have it either (Hans' comment about his sister's *wiwimacher*). It seemed that the phallus was nowhere to be found; wherever he thought it was, it was always elsewhere. Then who was it that really had it? Lacan proposes that there comes a turning point in the Oedipus complex, after which this imaginary object can no longer be used by the subject as a lure. The subject, at this point, must be shown that this object is with the Other, that the subject has no access to it, and that the subject "has it insufficiently", meaning the subject lacks this imaginary object, this imaginary phallus (p. 239). For Lacan, this is the crucial role that castration plays in the Oedipus complex. The subject must be deprived of this object in the "Oedipal experience", deprived by the "one who has it, who knows who has it, who has it in every instance" (p. 239). It is through this deprivation and this assumption that the child "can conceive that this same symbolic object will one day be given to him" (p. 239). It is the symbolic father who deprives the child and helps him conceive that he might have it in future, but what about the real father? What role has he? "I beg you to accept for the moment . . . in the Oedipal drama, it is to the real father that the salient function in the castration complex is effectively deferred" (Lacan, 1957, p. 253).

As the above quote suggests, for Lacan, the real father's intervention is crucial and the meaning of this comment can be grasped only when the discussion focuses on how castration operates. But first, let us examine what castration is for Lacan, as evident in these two lectures.

What is castration? The sign of the oedipal drama

It is evident that Lacan perceives the greatest problem for Freud in formulating the Oedipus complex as the question of "what is a father?" (p. 247). Lacan's own reformulation of the castration complex can be seen as centred around two particular aspects: the child's puzzlement around the question of femininity, the absence of the penis, which is similar to Freud's own puzzlement, as described in the previous chapters, and "What the child really is for the mother" (Lacan, 1957, p. 260), which is both a question of femininity in its maternal form and an elaboration of Freud's theory of penis envy.

In other words, the absence of a penis in the female body is also a major question for Lacan in formulating the theories of psychosexual development, just as it was for Freud. However, the major difference between Lacan's and Freud's theories lies in the very notion that Lacan opens up in the discussion by conceptualising the absence of the penis as a lack which can be interpreted in three registers: symbolic, imaginary, and real. In terms of the absence of the penis, Lacan uses the term "privation", which is the real lack. The notion of privation rests on what the male subject apprehends in the real "of the absence of the penis in women", that is, women's deprivation of the penis (Lacan, 1957, p. 250). Castration is at the base of this apprehension. The male subject's experience of this real lack is, as Lacan suggests, "effective and anxiety-provoking" (p. 250). Since the male subject perceives women's deprivation as their being castrated in the real, according to Lacan, privation is the symbolisation of the object in the real (discussed again in Chapter Seven). This realisation is also in line with Freud's theory of castration.

At the pre-oedipal stage, Lacan notes that castration is the taking away of an imaginary object and incurring a symbolic debt or a symbolic punishment and the inscription of this lack in the symbolic chain (p. 252). The symbolic chain can be understood at this stage as language, or the generation, or the human race, all of which pre-date the subject. The subject is born into language and has to find a way to be a part of it or not. Similarly, the family pre-dates the subject and the subject is situated in it. This "situating" of the subject is the placing of the subject in the symbolic, which is one of the aims of analysis. However, for the subject to be part of that "chain", there has to be the beginning of the construction of the subjective symbolic. This is where the symbolic father is the necessary agent, because such construction can only be achieved through a "mythical construction" (p. 252), since the symbolic father is nowhere to be found except in myths. For Lacan, Freud's formulation of the primal father in his *Totem and Taboo* is in line with this symbolic father. It is the primal father who was killed (p. 241), for the dead father is more powerful than the live one (Freud, 1912–1913, p. 143). Freud explains that after the jealous, castrating father was killed by the sons, they felt guilt and remorse. The sons declared killing, incest, and substituting the father forbidden. Freud described it as the case of "deferred obedience" (1912–1913, p. 143). Thus, Freud noted that "the dead father became stronger than the living one had been . . ." (1912–1913, p. 143). Lacan suggests that Freud's difficulties were around this notion of the father to begin with and that Freud aimed at arriving at this notion of the guaranteeing father by formulating this myth of the primal father. Hence, Freud's intervention in Hans' case consisted of the installation of a myth, since the real father could not acquire a position wherein he could transpose the imaginary phallus to the order of the symbolic. Myths, thus, play a crucial role in the formation of subjectivity.

However, it can be asked, if the symbolic father is the dead father and yet his presence is powerful, why did Freud's myth only push Hans into the oedipal drama but not bring his crisis to an end? First, it must be acknowledged that, for Freud, neurosis is a matter of choice: the "choice of neurosis" (Freud, 1913i), which means that Hans' choice of neurosis indicates something about his subjectivity, which is a debate that is ongoing. However, it is when faced with this question that one begins to appreciate Lacan's quote above, where he emphasises the intervention of the real father. Lacan highlights that it is the real father and not the symbolic or the imaginary one that has a significant role in the effectiveness of the castration complex. This is because, unlike the seduction theory that Freud brought to our attention (discussed in Chapter Five), castration is not a fantasy. For castration to be effective and be a significant part of the subject's history, it has to be linked to an incident where the real father intervenes (pp. 253–254), although such an effect can also be achieved by the absence of the real father, because it is how the father is spoken of that is important. This is also applicable for situations where someone else acts as the father. In order to grasp *how* the real father's intervention is crucial for castration to be effective, one needs to examine why castration is necessary. For example, why was an intervention necessary for Hans?

Why castration? Stuck in the imaginary

Hans' questions were not just related to his peepee-maker, but to all creatures' peepee-makers, and especially those of his parents. He was caught up in a game of comparison that is organised around the "model of the lure" and the maternal image for him was his double, rather an enlarged double (p. 236). This specular dialectic between the subject and the small other that is the mother stagnated the dialectic of the Oedipus complex in the imaginary and prevented the dialectic's promotion to the realm of the symbolic. The mother here is the lower-case other and not the upper-case Other because she is not really perceived by Hans as an other at all. She is, rather, a reflection of Hans and a projection of Hans' ego. This is evident in Hans' identification with the mother where he adopts imaginary children at the pre-phobic stage. For Freud, this is where symptoms emerge and, for

Lacan, this is the manifestation of anxiety. However, Lacan warns that anxiety is not to be equated with phobia; rather, the phobic object is to be understood as functioning in order to protect the subject from anxiety (p. 236). But what anxiety was Hans facing?

Trouble in paradise

In the pre-oedipal stage, the child perceives the mother as the symbolic mother, who nourishes, satisfies, and is the object of the child's love. It is only when she frustrates the child that the mother is perceived as the real mother. Although one of the fundamental experiences of the child is his ability to place himself as the object of the mother's love, too much love and too much dependency causes turmoil. If the child is the mother's sole love object and the mother is his, then not only is there no room for other relationships, but also there is pressure on the child to sustain himself as *the object that she lacks*: the imaginary phallus for the mother. In the pre-phobic phase, Hans considered this imaginary relation as the state of paradise, but that would change. In other words, as discussed above, for Lacan, in the pre-oedipal stage, the third element circulating in the relation between the mother and the child is the imaginary phallus. Lacan suggests that the child perceives the mother's desire and attempts to be that which she lacks: the imaginary phallus. Referring to Freud's penis envy, Lacan suggests that whether the child fulfils the mother's longing for the lost penis or not, penis envy is retained by women to various degrees. Lacan said, "It is the fact that, to a degree which differs among subjects, the mother still retains a *Penis-neid*" (1957, p. 257). Hans' mother's excessive attachment to Hans can be seen as the mother placing Hans as the compensation for the lost penis. For Lacan, *Penis-neid* is "one of the fundamental givens of analytic experience, and as a constant reference in the relation of the mother with the child" (1957, p. 258). In this regard, what is to be questioned in the light of the concept of penis envy is the mother's relation to the child, that is, the way she treats the child. *Penis-neid* is the only possible "way to explain the perversions" in hand, suggests Lacan.

Notice how Lacan uses "perversions" in its plural form. This is because Hans placed himself not only as the child who completes his mother, but also as the object of the mother's desire (1957, p. 258).

This, as Lacan points out, is the "relation of the fetishist to his object" (p. 258). However, it is important to highlight that, at the pre-oedipal stage, the "perversions" as Lacan puts it here, can neither be explained completely nor be generalised. But the decisive point is *what the child is for the mother*, because it is in this relation to the mother that he experiences the phallus and chooses to either *be the phallus* or *have the phallus*. Hence, for Lacan, in the negotiation of the Oedipus complex, when the subject is faced with castration, he chooses a position in relation to the phallus of being or having. It is this positioning of one's self in relation to the phallus that is to be understood as the subject's choosing a position as a sexual being (discussed again in Chapter Seven). In relation to the question of perversion, in this context it must be highlighted that perversion does not *cause* anxiety, it is a *response to* a specific anxiety: the castration anxiety. Both phobia and fetish are centred around this fundamental anxiety (p. 17).

Hans experienced anxiety when his penis became real. Hans could neither explain nor control the source of sensation, as he thought it came from outside. Anxiety, however, is not the same as fear, because anxiety has no object and that was precisely the problem. What Hans experienced was difficult to symbolise: it was real, was without an object, and, hence, he required something belonging to the symbolic, something he could organise his symbolic world around, something that could help him to make sense of things. Lacan explains that anxiety is the suspension of the subject between "a time in which he no longer knows where he is" and a fast approaching time where he will lose himself in a way that he will never find himself again (p. 260). This previous game of lure, where the penis was the source of happiness, a state of paradise, now, for Hans, becomes a trap, as the drive intervenes and the organ becomes real. Now Hans becomes what he is not and, rather, everything that his mother wants. Lacan describes this shift in Hans' position with regard to his mother as "the point of encounter with the real drive and the imaginary game of phallic lure" (p. 262). At this point, Lacan suggests that "regression is produced" (p. 262), and by "regression" he means that the same breast that was once the source of satisfaction now represents the devouring mother. This element of devouring, for Lacan, is a usual characteristic of phobia and which is evident in Hans' object of phobia: a horse that bites.

Function of the phobia

Hans was "bathed in happiness"; he was admitted as the third into the conjugal bed and truly he was frustrated by nothing, deprived of nothing. While his father was the most tolerant man, his mother seems to be the organiser and the decision-maker in the family. Hans' father neither took up the position of the guarantor, nor displayed his position as the possessor of the phallus. The pronouncement of his mother's threat that she would have Dr A come and cut off his penis if Hans continued to masturbate is not to be considered as a decisive moment for the formation of the phobia, but, rather, this incident served as the necessary material for the construction of the castration complex (p. 255). For Freud, it is where Hans acquired the castration complex and it operated via deferred effect. But why was this construction necessary? The phobia served to substitute for the function that Hans' father lacked, "the objects [in phobia] have a very special function . . . a stand in for the signifier of the symbolic father" (Lacan, p. 263).

Just as "paranoia branches out" (p. 261) at the point where the child becomes captive in the game that previously used to be of lure, and just as the material for delusions is not foreign but, rather, belong to the subject's history, similarly, phobia, too, is produced as a solution to a problem and the material of phobia is not foreign either. The phobic object essentially belongs to the subject's symbolic order. Hans' "encounter with the real drive and the imaginary game of phallic lure . . . with regard to his mother" produced a phobia in which the devouring of the mother can be seen in the horse that bites. The theme of "devouring" is always to be found in the structure of a phobia (p. 262). In this sense, for Lacan, the objects of phobia are borrowed signifiers. They also contribute to the analogy between the primal father and the totem that Freud articulated in *Totem and Taboo*: a signifier standing-in for the dead or the absent symbolic father.

The development of phobia does not belong to the imaginary, but to the symbolic. It is, rather, a solution to the imaginary problem in hand where a game of lure transforms into a trap and the dialectic of the mother–phallus–child relation becomes stagnated. The borrowed signifier, thus, opens up a pathway to the symbolic order where an organisation of the symbolic world can take place. At a critical moment of the pre-oedipal stage, when no other path is open for the solution to the problem, phobia attempts to rescue the subject.

Phobia is, thus, "an appeal to a singular symbolic element" which is also mythical in nature (p. 56), because this horse bites (i.e., intervenes like the castrating primal father in Freud's mythology). If the father is sufficiently there, "maintaining a sufficient distance between the three terms of the relation 'mother–child–phallus'", then the subject does not have to maintain the relation by giving something of his or her own (Lacan, 1957, p. 78). In that case, there might not be a need for producing phobias to serve the function of the symbolic father.

How does castration have an effect? Imaginary orgy, /intervention of the real father, and symbolic castration

In describing the phobia of a little English girl in this Seminar IV, Lacan suggested that the castrating animal in her dream was the essential element of articulation that allowed the little girl to pass through the crisis she entered as she was faced with maternal *impotence* (p. 77). In Hans' case, he was faced with maternal *omnipotence* and the phobia was Hans' attempt at organising his symbolic world. In Hans' case, the symbolic father was Freud, but his installation of the myth did not accomplish castration. Lacan presupposed that it is the real father who is the prominent agent in the castration complex, but Hans' real father hardly ever intervened (p. 253). He neither frustrated nor deprived Hans of anything. When the real father did finally intervene, he was "able to do so only because he has had behind him the symbolic father, who was Freud" (p. 264). Referring to the episode after the real father's intervention, Lacan noted that Hans reconstructed the presence of Hannah. This reconstruction is Hans' way of incorporating the father in the dilemma of the "origin of babies" (discussed in Chapter One), which previously contained no element of his father. There was a shift in Hans: from Hans' identification with his mother, his various forms of love relations with his playmates, and his imaginary adoption of children to his reconstruction of the theory of birth. For example, he spoke of other children as "my little girls" (Freud, 1909b, p. 15). While the prior position is denoted as the "imaginary orgy", Lacan aligns the later with the real father's intervention (p. 264). Hans' phobia ended not because of the symbolic father's intervention (Freud's myth) but because of the real father's intervention. The real father is not to be understood as the biological father, but one who is considered the father. He is an effect of language, the real of language (Evans, 1996, p. 63). His intervention is both crucial to, and independent of, his physical presence or absence. While Freud's installation of the myth aimed at helping Hans to transition from the pre-oedipal to the oedipal dialectic, it was the real father's intervention that led to the symbolic castration of Hans.

The dream of the plumber expresses such castration in the clearest form. The dream can be interpreted as someone from outside came and replaced what was real by something that was bigger and better. Phobia is, thus, associated to this triad of the "imaginary orgy, intervention of the real father and symbolic castration" (p. 265). Castration, in this case, brought phobia to an end, but it also helped Hans to conceive both the idea of replacement itself (the process of substitution) and the object of replacement (deprivation through castration and hope for the future). Thus, castration, for Lacan, not only brings the Oedipus complex to an end, but it also opens the pathway to the symbolic for the subject and, paradoxically, provides protection.

To sum up, this chapter examined two lessons from Lacan's Seminar IV and outlined *what* the castration complex is for Lacan, *why* it was necessary for Hans, and *how* it had its effect. As is evident from this exploration, for Lacan, the castration complex is played out entirely in the imaginary. The symbolic father who possesses the phallus is placed outside this imaginary, so that the intervention becomes somewhat convenient. This is because the intervention of the symbolic father comes from outside the mother–child relationship, from somewhere beyond the mother, with its prohibition and inscription of the law which assists the subject in constructing his symbolic world. But, at the same time, this inscription of law provides the child with a view of the future. In Lacan's theory, becoming a male or female sexed subject begins with the child assuming the phallus as a signifier that governs the symbolic chain, the genealogy of the human clan. Hence, for Lacan, it is the giving up of the child's position as the imaginary phallus in the hope of receiving it some day in the symbolic. Castration, for Lacan, is always of the imaginary phallus, but never of the real penis. Castration is, thus, a symbolic loss of an imaginary object whose agent is the real father. Yet, since "what is a father?" remains a source of puzzlement for all, it is only through mythical constructions that the symbolic father can be seen as a guarantor. It is on this notion of these puzzlements that the next chapter will examine Lacan's theories further.

CHAPTER SEVEN

The fate of infantile sexual research questions

Introduction

Just one year before Seminar IV, the lectures Lacan delivered in 1955–1956 during two academic terms were put together as a text titled, "On a question prior to any possible treatment of psychosis" (Lacan, 2006a). There, Lacan outlines Freud's theoretical framework in the following way. This description of Freud's framework will, in some ways, seem recognisable as it has been covered in this book so far. Lacan asserts that

> Freud maintains of the imaginary function of the phallus in the two sexes ... the castration complex to be a normative phase of the subject's assumption [*assomption*] of his own sex, the myth of the killing of the father rendered necessary by the constitutive presence of the Oedipus complex in every personal history. (p. 455)

all of which have been illustrated in the previous chapters. Lacan continues to highlight the Freudian framework, such as Freud's theories of the refinding of the object, the drive theory, and the "disjunction" between the aim, direction, and its object, which has also been described in the previous chapters. Finally, Lacan mentions a theory that is worth mentioning for the particular purpose in hand. Lacan refers to Freud's theory of drive and "its original 'perversion'" and the involvement of this perversion in the organisation of the libido "under the heading of the sexual theories of children" (Lacan, 2006a, p. 455). It is crucial to highlight that it is a perverse position with which we begin our life. Infantile sexuality is polymorphously perverse. It is due to the demands made upon the subject by society and civilisation that libidinal organisation shifts from this perverse position. Castration is to be considered one of these demands. In this chapter, I outline how these demands force the child to give up the infantile beliefs and what is the final fate of the infantile sexual research questions.

The previous chapter has already outlined how Lacan described castration as a symbolic act that invokes a lack of an imaginary object. This lack is necessary for the instalment of the subject in the symbolic chain because only when this debt is incurred does the subject find a place in this chain. He becomes a part of the wider world that is beyond the mother–child dyad. In order to gain something, one has to give something. Something that one never had to begin with, "to give one's love, is very precisely and essentially to give as such nothing of what one has, because it is precisely in so far as one does not have it that there is question of love" (Lacan, 1958, S5, p. 282). This acceptance of not having it to begin with is what Lacan theorises as castration. However, this "acceptance" might not always occur, and even when it does occur, it is not without its own difficulties. Moreover, we can question, whether it is lost or whether it is given up, do we get it back in future?

The theories of becoming a man or a woman in Lacan's work are extremely complex, at times seeming even more obscure than Freud's. Yet, the only way to understand Lacan's work is by reading it over and over again. The aim in this chapter will be to simplify a few foundational ideas on which Lacan's theories are based, without compromising their essence, and providing a brief theoretical picture of the subject in hand: what can we learn from Lacan's theory of castration about the subject's acquisition of sex? Acknowledging the complexity, density, and vastness of Lacan's work, this chapter will once again confine itself to three texts on the signification of the phallus, and occasional remarks will be drawn from Seminar III (1955–1956) and Seminar V (1957–1958).

On the signification of the phallus

Considering the depth and brevity of this lecture, we will confine our discussion to the first two paragraphs of the lecture. In this lecture from 1958, one year after the seminar on object-relation (Seminar IV), Lacan speaks of the function of the castration complex in the unconscious. His opening lines have some of the most assertive, definitive, and clear remarks on the topic of castration. It is worth studying them in parts to closely observe what Lacan is interpreting as the castration complex. Lacan asserts, "we know that the unconscious castration complex functions as a knot ..." (2006b, p. 575), which means that castration complex works at the level of the unconscious and it serves the function of a "knot", meaning it holds some things together. Lacan isolates two instances where the castration complex functions as a knot: "in the dynamic structuring of symptoms ... of what is analyzable in the neurosis, perversion and psychoses"; and

> in regulating the development that gives its *ratio* to this first role: namely, the instating in the subject of an unconscious position without which he could not identify with the ideal type of his sex or even answer the needs of his partner in sexual relations ... much less appropriately meet the needs of the child who may be produced thereby. (Lacan, 2006b, p. 575)

This suggests that the castration complex not only operates at the level of the formation of the symptoms and at the level of the very structuring of the subject, but it also helps the subject take up a sexual position from where he is able to "answer the needs" of his sexual partner and his future progeny. Based on our reading so far from the previous chapters and in the light of these comments of Lacan, it can be argued that symptoms reveal a lot about the subject's reaction to castration and the development of the following questions are regulated by the unconscious castration complex: the question of one's sex, the question of one's partner's sex, the question of procreation, including what it is to be a father and what the child is to the mother.

However, we might question why it is that the subject's assumption of the "attributes of that sex" depends on a "threat" or a "deprivation" (Lacan, 2006b, p. 575). Lacan suggests that reduction of the matter to "biological data" will not provide us with the answers. The answer is demonstrated in "the myth underlying the structuring brought on by the Oedipus complex" (Lacan, 2006b, p. 576). We have already discovered in the previous chapter that the prohibition of incest is a myth that is superior in its power, precisely because the primal father is dead. The symbolic father can be accessed only through myths. Myths paved the way to the symbolic order, and the subject's access to this symbolic order depends on the subject's submission to the laws inscribed by the myths. In order to submit to this law, the child gives up an imaginary identification with the phallus and begins to perceive the phallus in the symbolic. In this structuring of the Oedipus complex, it is through myths that the phallus can be symbolised by the child because the phallus operates as a signifier. It is at this level, the level of the signifier, which is not to be conflated with linguistics or cultural construction, but is, at the level of one's unconscious, governed by a law that is similar to language, that Lacan says one is to be deprived.

From Seminar V

In the same year as the text above was published, Lacan explains the following in a lecture dated 12 March 1958, found in Seminar V. In the dialectic process of the Oedipus complex, Lacan asserts that the function of the phallus as a signifier ϕ is to introduce the subject "to his existence, and to his sexual position"; it is through this fundamental signifier that "the desire of the subject has to make itself recognised as such, whether we are dealing with a man or dealing with a woman" (Lacan, 1958, S5, p. 198). This would imply that, irrespective of their biological sex, subjects have to position themselves in relation to this phallus, through which the subject's desire is constituted. The phallus is, thus, a reference point for whatever desire the subject might have. Yet, the importance lies in the following notions: that the subject "received his signification" himself, he holds "this power from a sign and that he only obtains this sign by mutilating himself of something through whose lack everything will take on a value" (Lacan, 1958, p. 198). In other words, there has to be a signification of the phallus, a signification that the subject makes himself, and this powerful signification must be held on to by the subject (as opposed to rejected), and will only occur if the subject offers a part of himself (i.e., becomes without something, without phallus "–φ", castrated). It is through the lack created by this imaginary mutilation that all other signification will take place. This first signification will be a phallic signification, all meaning from here on will be phallic, and, thus, the subject will become a sexed subject.

The subject's relation to the phallus
irrespective of anatomical distinction

In "Analysis terminable and interminable" (1937c), Freud linked the limitation of the castration complex to his clinical observation of a biological bedrock. This is a similar observation to that which Freud described in Lecture XXXIII "Femininity" (1933a). In "Femininity" (1933a) Freud described the phenomenon of the male's apparent openness to further change (in analysis) and women's psychical rigidity regarding the same as the variation of capacity to sublimate and concluded that women have less capacity to sublimate (see Chapter Five). In "Analysis terminable and interminable" (1937c), Freud described the rigidity in both in a different way, in the form of resistance. He described that it seems impossible "to convince a man that a passive attitude to men does not always signify castration" and to help a woman give up on her "wish for a penis" (Freud, 1937c, p. 252). The presence of castration anxiety in men's unconscious and penis envy in women's thus seems to Freud to be the biological bedrock of human subjects.

In his text, "The signification of the phallus" (2006b, pp. 575–576), Lacan refers to both this inherent feeling of loss in the psyche of the human subjects emphasised by Freud and the difficulties Freud experienced in theorising female sexuality. Lacan replaces the term penis with phallus, proposes that it should be considered as a signifier, and suggests that there is a relation between the subject (of either sex) and the phallus, "these facts reveal a relation between subject and the phallus that forms without regard to the anatomical distinction between the sexes and that is thus especially difficult to interpret in the case of women . . ." (2006b, p. 576). If one is to argue that the phallus is, in fact, the male organ, the penis, and it is *not* a signifier, then how are these following conundrums that Freud outlined in his doctrine to be understood?

How can we explain the little girl's belief that she has been castrated by her mother (even if this belief is transient)? Why would she consider that the mother, with whom she first identified, deprived her of a "phallus" and then identify with her father, which seems like a "transference in the analytic sense of the term" (Lacan, 2006b, p. 576)?

Why do both sexes consider their mothers to have the "phallus"; in other words, why is it that the mother is perceived as a "phallic mother" by both the little girl and the little boy (Lacan, 2006b, p. 576)?

Why is it that "the signification of castration in fact takes on its (clinical manifest) full weight in the formation of symptoms only on the basis of its discovery as the mother's castration" (Lacan, 2006b, p. 576)? In other words, it is the children's (both sexes) perception of their mother's castration where the meaning of castration unfolds and, hence, it is *this* perception of the mother (her status with regard to castration) that contributes to the formation of symptoms: but why (Lacan, 2006b, p. 576)?

In Freud's theory, the emphasis lies on the phallic phase, which is to be understood as "the first genital maturation" phase, where the "imaginary dominance of the phallic attribute" and "masturbatory jouissance" localised in the clitoris raises the clitoris to the function of the phallus (2006b, p. 576). First, one can ask why Freud emphasises the clitoris in this phallic phase and, second, why he excludes "any instinctual mapping of the vagina as the site of genital penetration" in both sexes, instead postponing it until a later stage of development (Lacan, 2006b, p. 576).

Lacan highlights that, in Freud's work, one can already see the play of a signifier and a signifiable succumbing "to its mark" as a signified, even though modern linguistic analysis postdates Freud (2006b, p. 578). The answers to these questions indicate that there *is* a signifier in play, which predates the subject, which "becomes a new dimension of the human condition", where not only man speaks, but also "in man and through man that it *qua* speaks" (2006b, p. 578). Lacan believes this is where one begins to notice the connection between the phallus and the subject, a relationship that is established due to the castration complex without regard to the subject's biological sex. Further, one can ask, how does Lacan reformulate the Freudian theory of penis envy in the light of his proposal that the phallus is a signifier?

Lacan's revision of penisneid *in Seminar V*

In Freud's theory of female psychosexual development, we have learnt that there are three pathways that lead her to the Oedipus complex and, hence, there are three outcomes after the girl discovers the difference between the sexes. Lacan perceives these three modes in relation to the phallic phase and highlights three different meanings of penis envy, which he refers to in German as *penisneid*. The first meaning of *penisneid* is in the sense of a phantasy, which is also a wish "that the clitoris is a penis" (Lacan, 1958, p. 201). The second meaning is where *penisneid* intervenes and frustrates the girl. The girl desires her father's penis, but she realises that the Oedipus complex prohibits her from having access to her father's penis and also that it is a physical impossibility that she can have it. Lacan believes this is where "the situation has frustrated her" (Lacan, 1958, p. 201). The third situation is where *penisneid* develops in the little girl "the phantasy of having a child by her father", which Lacan refers to as a wish of "having this penis in a symbolic form" (Lacan, 1958, p. 201).

At this stage in the text, Lacan reminds us of the three kinds of lack that he introduced us to in his Seminar IV (1956–1957) in relation to the castration complex: castration, frustration, and privation. He now explains that "frustration is something imaginary directed towards an object that is quite real" (Lacan, 1958): the girl receiving her father's penis and the prohibition of the Oedipus complex is a situation that frustrates her, marking a lack. The third situation of *penisneid* correlates with the lack referred to as privation by Lacan. This is because privation is "real", and "is only directed towards a symbolic object" (Lacan, 1958, p. 201). Privation, though, is a lack in the real and, by definition, the real does not lack. Privation is the symbolisation of the object in the real (Lacan, 1957, p. 54). The object here is to have a child from her father, a child that is a symbol that is lacking and frustrating her. Her symbolisation of this object that is lacking in the real and her "desire for the father's child", hence, indicate that the lack in question, in this instance, is privation (Lacan, 1958, p. 201).

Castration, on the other hand, is when the subject is "symbolically" cut "off from something imaginary, and in this instance from a phantasy" (Lacan, 1958, p. 201). Lacan agrees with Freud in this instance, where Freud suggested that "she must renounce this clitoris at least in so far . . . as a sign of hope" that soon, one day, "it would become something as big as a penis" (Lacan, 1958, p. 201). It is structurally at this level that Lacan says "the phallus intervenes here *qua* signifier" (Lacan, 1958, p. 202). He proposes that this relation with regard to the clitoris is not a "defensive formation", as Jones suggested in the famous psychoanalytic debate on feminine sexuality, and it is also not comparable to phobia (Lacan, 1958, p. 203). Rather, the intervention of the phallus serves a different role here, "the phallus plays the role of the fetish" (Lacan, 1958, p. 203).

It would be useful to remind ourselves of the difference between the fetish object and the phobic object. The fetish object is a "symbolic substitute for the mother's missing phallus", whereas the phobic object is an "imaginary substitute for symbolic castration" (Evans, 1996, p. 64). Considering the brevity and density of the topic of desire in Lacan's theory, I shall highlight only two aspects for further consideration at this juncture. First, if the clitoris acts as a symbolic substitute for the missing penis, and if clitoral enjoyment is not given up in exchange for the new chief erotogenic zone, the vagina, then theoretically this is to be considered as the clitoris acting as a fetish object, acknowledging that, clinically, this is not to be considered as a correlation, as that would imply that a symptom is being considered as a sign, which is *not* a psychoanalytic approach. Second, it can be argued that even when clitoral enjoyment is given up and the wish for a child has replaced the wish for a penis, the child herself can act as a fetish object to the mother. This is a tendency also presented by Lacan in his Seminar V lecture dated 23 April (1958, p. 269). It can be added that it is this inclination that led Lacan to investigate Hans' phobia in relation to fetishism and to describe the situation as "perversions", not "perversion" (see Chapter Six). It can be also added that, based on my second observation, females can be theorised as fetishists in the psychoanalytic sense precisely because the phallus is a signifier. While the phobic might feel suffocated by attempting to continue as the mother's phallus, the fetishist will try everything to perceive the mother with a phallus. Either way, the common factor in both fetish and phobia is the concept of a mother with a phallus. This is a perception about human sexuality which is impossible to grasp by investigating it through the disciplines of anatomy, biology, sociological, psychological, or any other school of thought precisely because the workings of field of the mental can be accessed only via psychoanalytic investigation.

If the phallus is a signifier, what is the signified?

So far, it is evident that the phallus, for Lacan, is the role that the male genital plays in the phantasy of the subjects of both sexes (Evans, 1996, p. 140). The doctrines of the object-relation school might describe the phallus as a part-object, or a good or a bad object, but Lacan opposes this view (2006a, p. 463). Rather, Lacan perceives it as an imaginary object and, because he theorises the phallus as a signifier, it can be added that Lacan perceives the phallus as symbolic object, too. However, if the phallus is a signifier, where is the signified, we might ask. In his Seminar V, during a lecture on 15 January 1958, Lacan clarifies that looking for the answer "at the centre of object relations is pure stupidity" (1958, p. 125). Rather, the child himself (and here again the sex of the child is immaterial) is a part object. The child is an appendage, an extension of the mother. This is the pre-Oedipus stage, where it is not yet clear where the child ends and where the mother begins. Hence, the child wonders, "What does this mean, her coming and going?" (1958, p. 125). Is it not *me* that she wants always? Is it not *me* that satisfies her completely? Is there *something else* that she wants? *What* does she want? Lacan says, "this signified of comings and goings of the mother, is the phallus" (1958, p. 125). Now, the child can try to be that which satisfies her mother elsewhere, and, in that case, the child is trying *be* the phallus. The child wants to *be* what she is lacking, the phallus for the mother; that is, the child wants to fill her lack. But do we ever know what the "that" she wants is? It is impossible to know what the other wants, but the very fact that I will never know what exactly the other wants will keep me guessing, keep me desiring, keep me looking for the answers. I can keep trying to *be* that or *have* that. Hence, castration marks the subject with a lack that causes him to desire, gives him hope for future, and gets him going at the very beginning. Even though "that" will always escape symbolisation, will always stay out of one's reach, it is the journey itself that will save the subject from disappearing into nothing, the real.

But what if there was no "coming and going" of the mother? What if there was nothing for one to guess, to figure it out? What if everything was right there, for example, excessive attentiveness and no space for frustration (both child and mother)? Or what if nothing was there, for example, a mother who is suffering and cannot engage with the child at all? In reality, in the early days and months of the child's life, it is the mother or the primary carer who is always there with the child. The mother is considered by both the sexes in their early phase as someone who does not lack anything. While it is essential that the mother provides security, love, and affection, it is also important that the child recognises that he/she does not *complete* her, that there is more that the mother desires; in other words, that she lacks *something*. This significant time in the Oedipus complex, for Lacan, can be described the first "time" of the Oedipus complex. On the other hand, it is important to remember that the mother–child bond is crucial for the child's development and a child might perceive it as a failure on his part if the mother is not satisfied by the child. Too much presence of the mother is as problematic as too much absence of the mother. Both the absence and the presence are to be understood as emotional, as expressed in her actions and speech. It is not her physical absence or presence that is in question here.

Therefore, the lack in question is to be understood in relation to the child's first introduction to the law. It is only when the child perceives that a law is imposed on the mother, denying her access to her enjoyment of this phallic object that the child poses himself as, and, at the same time, the law is imposed on the child, forbidding his access to his mother, that we can refer to the situation as the second time of the Oedipus complex for Lacan. Lacan refers to this phenomenon as the castration of the mother, but he also describes it as privation. For the child to perceive this lack in the mother, he would first have to symbolise the phallus and then perceive it as missing and, hence, Lacan suggests that privation is a lack in the real, as in reality there is something missing in the mother: she does not have the phallus (Lacan, 1957, p. 53). For this privation to take place there has to be the image of the father, the imaginary father, which can be the father himself but also it can be the law imposed on the mother and child by someone else, or something else. The emphasis is, however, placed on the fact that the mother obeys this law and the child perceives the mother as succumbing to this law. For instance, there can be a real father or another adult who can impose laws on the mother and the child using verbal speech or action. Similarly, it can even be as subtle as, when a mother says, "I *have* to go to work/cook for . . .", or "you *have* to sleep in a different room", the very fact that she says she *has to* indicates that there is a force outside the mother–child dyad and the mother is obliged to obey its law. This is where the child begins to feel he is in rivalry with the agency that his mother is succumbing to and desiring. The mother's submission to this law must be perceived by the child through both the mother's words and her actions.

The meaning unfolding

The Oedipus complex in Lacan is not to be understood as a combination of chronological steps. As described in Chapter Six, this is a dialectic process. In this process, the meaning of the phallus unfolds. How we made sense of this phallus and how it was introduced to us will influence the very construction of our subjectivity. Lacan believes that the dialectic process of the Oedipus complex can essentially be described as a metaphor. A metaphorical process refers to the mechanism of substitution, which is similar to the construction of metaphor in linguistics, where one concept is understood in terms of another concept. The metaphoric process in the Oedipus complex consists of the following: the desire for the mother or the desire of the mother is replaced with the father's "no" or his name. Lacan calls this the paternal metaphor.

Name of the father. Desire of the mother _____ Name of the Father   A
Desire of the mother Signified to the subject.   Phallus

Through the matheme shown above, Lacan described the signification process involved in the paternal metaphor. The meaning produced in the matheme has the signified as the phallus and the signifier as A. A refers to the French *Autre*, in Lacan's terminology, this is to be understood as the capitalised Other. Considering the complexity of Lacan's algebraic concept A, for the purpose of this discussion, it would be useful for the moment to understand A as referring to the symbolic order, the language, and the law. Once this first metaphor is established, the meaning-making process begins and all future signification will, thus, be phallic from then on. The establishment of this first metaphor will be the foundation for the subject's structure (in Lacan's use of this term) and it will influence the subject's future object choices, both sexual and non-sexual. Lacan believes that the assumption of sexuality and object choice of the subject depend on this first establishment of the metaphor in the subject's psyche. But what would make him come to such a realisation? The answer can be found if we look closely at a structural level of how the paternal metaphor works and what it looks like when it does not work. In other words, it is useful to learn from the instance where the Oedipus complex is essentially incomplete, where, at a structural level, something did not function and created a hole, where, at the level of signification, there remains a fundamental lack: the structure of psychosis (Lacan, 1993, p. 201).

> It is an accident in this register and in what occurs in it—namely, the foreclosure of the Name-of-the-father in the place of the Other—and the failure of the paternal metaphor that I designate as the defect that gives psychosis its essential condition, along with the structure that separates it from neurosis. (Lacan, 2006a, p. 497)

Very briefly, in the Lacanian structure of psychosis, the name-of-the-father is foreclosed. The mechanism at the level of the constitution of one's subjectivity is known as foreclosure in Lacan's teachings. In other words, the formation of the "I" as a subject is fundamentally stunted. The father in psychosis is not perceived as a symbolic father and he is reduced to an imaginary father, an agent with whom the subject is in rivalry. The lack of this symbolic father is a crucial element in the structure of psychosis. Due to the absence of the symbolic father, there remains a hole in the symbolic where all signification fails. The phallic meaning is, thus, never achieved. The effect is a disturbance in the field of language of the subject, such as certainty, exact or literal meaning, neologism, inability to enjoy jokes, all of which affect the relationship of the subject to others. Moreover, the subject's sexual sphere is affected in the sense that his sexuality will never be realised or integrated in the symbolic plane (Lacan, 1993, p. 170). The manifestation of this was captured in Freud's case history of Schreber (Freud, 1911c).

Lack of a question in psychosis

Schreber wanted to experience sexual intercourse as a woman, believed that God was turning him into a woman, and that he was capable of giving birth. Without delving deep into the case history, as it would be beyond the scope of this book, and without describing the details of the psychoanalytic diagnostic features of psychosis, I shall highlight only one aspect of psychosis. Notice how Schreber's experience was *not* a question. Questions are formed when there is doubt and a doubt is formed when there is something missing or something seems different. The psychotic subject does not give up his position of being the maternal phallus. In other words, the subject did not submit to castration and, hence, there is nothing missing in psychosis. The psychotic lacks nothing. The mother–child dyad does not change into an Oedipal triangle. Hence, there is no place for doubt, no emergence of questions in psychosis, but only the statement "it is because it is". For Schreber, his phantasy was a matter of certainty, a matter of believing that the body is feminine, a body with a real orifice capable of giving birth (i.e., procreating). The phantasy of pregnancy in psychosis, a psychotic break triggered around the question of procreation and disturbances at the level of the subject's body, to the extent that there will be demands to have the genitalia surgically removed and/or having it replaced with that of the other sex can be considered clinical indicators of a psychotic structure in the Lacanian sense. However, these symptoms are *not* to be taken at face value and assumed to signal the presence of a psychotic structure. In that case, one would be approaching symptoms as signs, and the assumption of such a correlation is *not* a psychoanalytic approach. Also, it is important to highlight that surgical and non-surgical attempts to reconstruct or modify the body are not the same as demanding to change one's sex, believing with certainty that one *is* of a different sex. It is evident that, in the psychotic structure, the paternal metaphor is not established, signification of phallus does not take place, and the subject remains stuck in a dyad of the mother–child relation and caught up in the imaginary. Since there is no phallus, no symbolic father is there to claim the phallus. In psychosis, there is no one who imposes the law of sexuality and, hence, for the psychotic, there is no difference between the sexes precisely because he lacks nothing and for him there is no Other.

Questions in neurosis

The neurotic, on the other hand, has questions. Why is that the case? Speech belongs to the realm of the symbolic. The messages we receive and send through our speech are always aimed at the Other. But this

Other does not reply directly to us, and neither can we access this Other directly. By "we", I am referring to the neurotics, particularly the hysterics. The hysteric, thus, has to depend on the speech of the others (lower case) to make sense, which is the imaginary register, where social relations take place based on imaginary identifications. Hence, nothing the hysteric hears or learns or receives from around him will ever be enough, as the Other for the hysteric *does* exist and the hysteric is aware that he does not have access to it. However, hysterics are striving constantly to gain access to the Other and, temporarily, this access can be effected by granting the master's position to an agency. This could be the magazine that claims to teach one secret tricks to use in bed, how to look a certain way, how to be, or even suggests a surgery that can make one look like someone else, something else. Why this constant effort to reach out to the Other? Precisely because it is the Other who validates whether we are doing it right or not, whether we are behaving like a man or a woman should or not, whether we are feminine enough or masculine enough or not.

Hysterics require these validations, because, to begin with, it was the paternal metaphor where these validations were first made through the subject's introduction to the symbolic father. It is there, at the level of signification, that a metaphoric process took place to begin with; the subject accepted castration and repressed it. This acceptance of castration was made begrudgingly in hysterics, which is evident in their constant efforts *not* to accept the limits imposed on them by society, nature, authorities, or by others. However, the importance lies in the fact that the subject knows he or she is castrated (even though in revolts against this knowledge), and so is the mother who is also the first other. This mark of the fundamental lack is the very manifestation of dissatisfaction in hysterics. The hysteric is always missing something. The paternal metaphor in neurosis is, thus, repressed in the unconscious but does not stay there without causing commotion. The repressed returns in the form of symptoms; underlying these symptoms there are existential questions. Unlike psychotics, hysterics *do have* questions because they are fundamentally lacking and are marked by castration.

Lacan describes the hysteric's questions as "Who am I?", "What am I?", "Am I a man or woman?", "What is it to be a woman?", "Am I capable of procreating?" (Lacan, 1993, pp. 170–171). Lacan explains that these questions are "obviously located at the level of the Other, insofar as integration into sexuality is tied to symbolic recognition" (1993, p. 170). The subject recognises his sexual positions in the Oedipus complex and this recognition is "tied to the symbolic apparatus" (1993, p. 170). By "symbolic apparatus", Lacan means the "preformed" agency, something that predates the child, namely language, the symbolic, "that institutes the law in sexuality" (1993, p. 170). It is in this chain of "preformed" signifiers, the chain of the symbolic that both predates and postdates the child, that Lacan insists that "the subject has to find his place" (1993, p. 170). Since signifiers and signifieds are not stuck together, the meanings change, and, hence, there is always a possibility that the hysteric did not quite get it right. While this might explain domestic scenarios where a woman spends hours getting ready to go out, or even, as in Freud's case history of Dora, spending hours looking at the painting of the Madonna wondering "what is it to be a woman?", this is *not* the same dilemma as that of the psychotic that Lacan describes as the "feminised character" in psychosis. Feminisation in the psychotic structure is not a question. The psychotic does not get his messages coming via the (lower case) others. Unlike the neurotics, who spend their lives in doubt waiting to hear from the Other, which will never happen if all goes well, the psychotic hears it directly from the Other and he hears it crystal clear, there is no doubt about it.

Feminisation in psychosis

In psychosis, the signifiers for masculinity and femininity are almost blurred and the meaning of these terms almost melt into one another (Nobus, 2000, p. 19). This is precisely because no signification took place in the beginning at the level of the construction of the "I" as a subject. Castration, that is, the limitations, the imposition of laws of sexuality, the boundaries, the name-of-the-father, was foreclosed. It was never integrated within the subject's psyche. Although the "collapse of sexual differences" does not indicate the presence of a psychotic structure, *not* assuming "a shared sociocultural system of distinct sexual identities" and the subject "succumbing to a sexual matrix in which the boundaries between the categories have become very hazy" (Nobus, 2000, p. 20) *do* indicate the occurrence of chaotic experience within, the lack of symbolisation in the Oedipus complex, the absence of a symbolic father, and the dominance of an imaginary identification of the subject with the mother. Dora's question was "not on what sex she is, but *What is it to be a woman?*" (Lacan, 1993, p. 171). The hysteric's question, "Am I a man or a woman", is also asked by children in their infantile research into the matter of sex, which is *not* to be taken literally as, which sex am I? It is children who make this distinction and take this question literally and, thus, understand the difference between the sexes during the early years of their lives, as Freud described in his theories on infantile sexual researches (see Chapter One).

From a Freudian perspective, this first distinction between the sexes is equivalent to castration. If the same questions are raised in adulthood and one asks, "Am I a man or woman?", it is useful if it is interpreted in the way Lacan interprets Dora's question, "*What is it to be a woman? and, specifically, What is a feminine organ?*" (1993, p. 172). Because such interpretation leads us to a crucial discovery, "the woman wonders about what is it to be a woman, just as the male subject wonders about what is it to be a woman" (Lacan, 1993, p. 172). This discovery is an indication that there is a dissymmetry in the Oedipus complex between the two sexes (1993, p. 172), which means that female sexuality is indeed a mystery, even to women. However, this discovery does not explain the feminisation of a male subject with a psychotic structure. Can this feminisation be accounted for by the subject's imaginary identification with his mother in the absence of the phallus or the absence of a father in his early years? Or, rather, is there an imaginary relation of the subject to his father which is marked with hostility? Was there a "rivalrous, erotically charged tension" between the subject and the imaginary father that can explain the psychotic subject's feminisation (Fink, 1997, p. 99)? Lacan speaks of both these subjects in his Seminar III on psychosis. A particular teaching which addresses the subjects of (1) dissymmetry in the Oedipus complex and (2) feminisation in the psychotic structure is "The hysteric's question (II): What is a woman?" (Lacan, 1993, pp. 173–182). The findings from the reading of this text are outlined in the next section.

On the hysteric's questions from Seminar III

In this text, Lacan places emphasis on the distinction between the imaginary and the symbolic as it unfolds in Freud's work. The ego, in

Freud's writing, in a neurotic structure has the capability of "reality testing" (Lacan, 1993, p. 174). The ego creates a fantasy relation and strengthens the ego's existence. Reality, for the subject, is the ego's illusion, and this is "what Freud called ego-ideal" (1993, p. 174). The function of the ego ideal is not to experience the external world objectively, but to create an illusion. This function is "narcissistic" in nature and "it's on the basis of this function that the subject gives something its connotation of reality" (1993, p. 174). When a neurotic asks questions, he does so "with his ego". The neurotic's structure itself is a question, and the questions that the neurotic asks are, indeed, the questions of all of us, as they affect us all. Lacan illustrates that this is precisely what is demonstrated in Dora's question. While Dora was trapped in a "symptomatic state", Freud made the mistake of not highlighting Dora's "fundamental subjective duality" (1993, p. 174). The question, for Freud, should have been "who desires Dora", but, rather, Freud wondered "what Dora desires" (1993, p. 174). Dora's interest lies in Frau K and she identified with Herr K. Lacan believes that it is Herr K who was Dora's ego (p. 175). Dora was in an imaginary identification with Herr K. Similar to the specular image in the mirror stage, where for the first time the subject situates his ego, Dora identified with Herr K. In this identification, Dora *was* Herr K and in this way her symptoms made sense (1993, p. 175).

For Freud, Dora's aphonia, which used to occur only on Herr K's absence, was due to the fact that Dora did not have a need to talk during Herr K's absence as she can write to him. For Lacan, the oral symptoms have different explanation: Dora has "dried up", because "the mode of objectification hasn't been raised anywhere else" (1993, p. 175). In other words, in Herr K's absence, Dora is alone with Frau K and she is aware that her father's relation with Frau K involves fellatio. To Lacan, Dora's complaint about Herr K is a part of her wish to sustain Herr K as an object with which she identifies. Lacan points out that this is similar to the dialectic of the imaginary and the symbolic in the Oedipus complex (p. 175).

Lacan acknowledges that Freudian theories explain symptoms from a "structural plane", and by illustrating various common features Freud insisted that the Oedipus complex is essentially dissymmetrical in the two sexes (p. 175). Is this dissymmetry due to the child's first primitive love for the mother or is it because Freud outlined an "anatomical component" that "for the woman the sexes are identical" (1993, p. 175)? Referring to the Freudian texts (1923–1925) that we read closely in Chapter Two of this book, Lacan proposes that, in Freud's arguments, it is clear that "the dissymmetry is located at the symbolic level" and it is due to "the signifier" (p. 176). This is a unique revision of Freud's theories.

Lacan explains that there is no symbolisation of woman's sex (i.e., her genital). In the case of a man's genital, the process of symbolisation involves naming something that is present; the case of the woman does not involve the same process of symbolisation. In the imaginary, one can only notice the absence of something when "elsewhere there is a highly prevalent symbol" (p. 176). This phallic prevalence "forces the woman to take a detour via identification with the father" in the Oedipus complex, which means the girl has to follow the same path as the boy for a little while (p. 176). Similar to the boy, because of this prevalence of the imaginary phallus, via her father the girl, too, has access to the "oedipal complex" and "her imaginary identification" (p. 176). But this phallic *Gestalt* must itself be taken as a "symbolic element" that is at the centre of the Oedipus complex (p. 176). In other words, soon the imaginary phallus must become the symbolic phallus in the Oedipus complex.

Lacan clarifies the role of the castration complex in both sexes in relation to the phallus, the father, and the Oedipus complex in the following manner. He says, that for both the boy and the girl,

> ... the castration complex assumes a pivotal value in bringing about the Oedipus complex, and it does so precisely as a function of the father, because the phallus is a symbol to which there is no correspondent, no equivalent. It's a matter of a dissymmetry in the signifier. This signifying dissymmetry determines the path down which the Oedipus complex will pass. The two paths make them both pass down the same trail—the trail of castration. (p. 176)

This is, arguably, the most clear comment of Lacan in this whole seminar regarding the role of the phallus in the Oedipus complex and the centrality of the castration complex within the Oedipus complex. The way this signifier was realised by the subject before the Oedipus complex will affect the subject's experience within the Oedipus complex (p. 176). The girl has been both without the phallus and with the imaginary phallus before the Oedipus complex, and, hence, she can choose either a feminine position or a masculine position. Lacan explains something striking about this realisation of sexuality: "one of the sexes is required to take the image of the other sex as the basis of its identification" and this cannot be considered as "a pure quirk of nature" (p. 176). This comment refers to a regulation operating at the level of the symbolic, the level of the signifier.

Yet, if there is no symbolic material, there will be a major "obstacle, a defect, in the way of bringing about the identification that is essential for the subject's sexuality to be realised", according to Lacan (p. 176). It is evident that Lacan agrees that one assumes one's sexual position at the end of the Oedipus complex but he differs from Freud in the sense that this is an identification with the symbolic phallus, rather than the same-sex parent, as Freudian theory suggests. Where does this "defect" come from? Lacan says that the symbolic might lack "material" (p. 176). This could mean that, out of all the components that one needs for the Oedipus complex to take place, such as the father's presence, his intervention, the mother's submission, or something else, one of them or some them might be lacking. However, Lacan adds that "the female sex is characterised by an absence, a void, a hole, which means that it happens to be less desirable than in the male sex for what he has that is provocative, and that an essential dissymmetry appears" (p. 176).

How do we make sense of this comment? We have already read how Hans was hoping that his baby sister's *wiwimacher* will get bigger one day, so it must not be too hard to think of instances where a little girl might have expressed her wish to have as big an apparatus as her male siblings or playmates. The entire theory of penis envy depends on this assumption. However, Lacan clarifies that it is not just a matter of linking material, but, rather, it is a question of the "subject's relationship with the signifier as a whole" (p. 176). This is where again it must be highlighted that psychoanalytic investigation into human sexuality differs from other examination routes.

Lacan continues to make sense of the situation in the following way. It is the realm of the symbolic that opens the "entire world system" to a subject (p. 177). On the one hand, it seems that it is a man's level of knowledge that gives him the ability to name things. On the other hand, it seems, as a matter of "ethology, animal psychology", "the domain of the erotization of the object" (p. 177). The subject's acquisition of the sexual position is linked to his Oedipus complex, where the subject is first alienated, which makes him desire someone else's object, and then the subject "possess[es] it through the proxy of an other" subject (p. 177). It would be useful to remember Dora's identification with Herr K at this stage in order to understand this last comment. The Oedipus complex, for Lacan, is a traversal of a fundamentally symbolised relationship (p. 177). This indicates the primacy of the play of a signifier and signified, which would mean that, for the subject to take up his or her sexual position at the end of the Oedipus complex, the function of the man and woman has to be symbolised within the complex; for this to take place, one has to uproot these functions from the imaginary and place them in the symbolic, where they are either named or eroticised. If a genital realisation is not symbolised, then this process of symbolising the function of man and woman remains incomplete. Lacan suggests that this genital symbolisation is essential, "that the man be virilized, that the woman truly accept her feminine function" (p. 177).

Conversely, however, Lacan reminds us that it is in the imaginary order that humans identify with one another, that one relates to the other, and, based on this identification, an object becomes "an object of competition" (p. 177). It would be useful to think of the colloquial social expression, "I will have what she is having", where objects in the other's possession become desirable and it leads to competition. The domain of knowledge and the domain of the imaginary identification are counterparts of one another. Unlike the animal kingdom, humans have language and, hence, the human world is more enjoyable as these two domains interlink—"an object is isolated, neutralised, and as such particularly erotized" (p. 178). It is in this "interweaving" of the symbolic and the imaginary that Lacan suggests one finds "the source of the function that the ego plays in the structuring on a neurosis" (p. 178). It is crucial to highlight, here, that prioritising the register of the symbolic over the imaginary is a personal choice; this is *not* what psychoanalysis aims to teach (often trainees will hold such views). Both the realms are necessary for human functioning and the existence of the symbolic gives the human race the stamp of uniqueness in the animal kingdom. While the symbolic provides the subject with his entry into language, into the world of symbolisation, while the position of the analyst in analysis is to be from the place of the Other, the imaginary, on the other hand, is also an essential domain for several reasons. The development of human relations, social bonds, and, most of all, the establishment of the newborn's first relation with his mother depends on the subject's access to this imaginary domain. But how are we understand the role that this interweaving of the domains plays in the emergence of the neurotic's question?

Lacan explains that Dora's question *"What is a woman?"* can be interpreted as Dora's attempt to symbolise the female organ (p. 178). Since the man is the bearer of the penis, Dora's identification with a man is to be interpreted as Dora using the bearer of the penis as a means to get a grasp of this definition, which otherwise escapes her (p. 178). In other words, Dora is "literally using the penis as an imaginary instrument for apprehending what she hasn't succeeded in symbolizing" (p. 178). Lacan believes that, clinically speaking, there are more female hysterics than men purely because "the path to the woman's symbolic realization is more complicated" (p. 178). He then suggests that "becoming a woman" and "wondering what a woman is" are two different things (p. 178). Lacan argues that just because someone wonders about the definition of a woman, it does not mean that she becomes a woman and, similarly, wondering about a definition is opposed to becoming that (p. 178). The position of the woman is a problematic position; it involves a detour around one's "subjective realization" (i.e., the subject's own interpretation of the position) and, "up to a certain point it's unassimilable" (p. 178). This is where we begin to see Lacan's difficulty in theorising feminine sexuality; it is similar to Freud's, but the paths of investigation are slightly different. However, Lacan perceives the position of the woman as becoming most stable when it locks itself in the structure of hysteria. Hysteria being the simplest structure of all, it provides the least possible points of "rupture" (p. 178). Lacan believes that a woman usually begins to identify with her father as soon her question emerges with regard to the symbolisation of woman.

Lacan considers that the Oedipal realisation is better structured in masculine hysteria and that there is a lesser chance in a masculine hysteria for the neurotic's question to arise (p. 178). But of it does and when it does, the man, too, will question "what is it to be a woman?". This instance marks another dissymmetry between the sexes in the Oedipus complex: both sexes wonder about the feminine position and what it is like to be a woman (p. 178). Why is this the case? Is it really due to the difficulty in symbolising the female genital? Why do both Lacan and Freud seem not to get past the real hole that can be symbolised only by an absence of something that exists elsewhere?

At this stage in the text, Lacan reminds his reader of a case involving a fantasy of pregnancy in a young man aged thirty. Lacan explains that hysteria is known to have an effect on the subject's body that seems "fantasmatic" and "fragmenting", which remains unexplained by medical pathological investigation, and, hence, "it's always a question of an imaginary anatomy" in hysteria (p. 178). The common factor in feminine and masculine hysteria is not only the question of the feminine position, but also it is a question of procreation. The questions concerning giving birth, paternity, and maternity are not easily signified, symbolised, or reduced to signifiers, reduced to experience. Something of these terms always escapes language. Similar to the position of the woman, the question of procreation is a problematic one. In the question of paternity lies the question of the father and the function he serves. Lacan describes it in the following way.

It is the symbolic where the subject's being is located. He exists as a signifier, that is, he exists as a name. It is at this level of the language, in the realm of the symbolic, that he is recognised and he constructs his own myths, such as: I am this and I am that. In the chain of signifiers, each has a value, they are there for a reason, and they are connected. But what "evades the symbolic tapestry" is the question of procreation—"one being is born from another" (p. 179). How does one explain this new entry in the symbolic chain? No matter in how much detail one describes procreation, something will still manage to slip out, as if language fails to hold it all, to describe it all. Creation cannot be entirely explained by the symbolic (p.179).

Similarly, the symbolic does not have signifiers enough to explain death: "what is death?" Lacan reminds his reader that Freud has already highlighted this enigma in his *Beyond the Pleasure Principle* (1920g). The continuous reproduction of life can be seen as a life that is "forced to repeat the same cycle, rejoining the common aim of death" (Lacan, 1993, p. 179). In a similar way, Freud has illustrated how neurosis reproduces itself, following the signifier in a manner that the subject's relation to this signifier rises higher and higher (p. 179). The subject's relation to a signifier is unique and individual. His personal myths, what he is, where has he come from, where he is going, all of this will be the subject's own construction put together using signifiers. This is something Lacan will later describe as the fundamental phantasy, which is not discussed in this book. However, notice how, in this process, the signifiers do not give him the answers, it is *he* as a subject who constructs them. To the signifiers, to the symbolic, to language, his life or death or sex is irrelevant unless he symbolises them and makes them exist in language. Only when subjects have realised themselves as a man or a woman in the symbolic do the questions of procreation and death arise. If this realisation of one's sex has not been symbolised, or brought to the level of the symbolic, then there will remain a hole and the questions of death or procreation will not be tolerated by the subject, which might instigate a sudden psychotic break. The questions raised by hysterics are similar to that of psychotics, and this is precisely why Lacan brought up the questions of hysteria in his seminar on psychosis.

Tolerance

Neurotic structure is a question itself, as Lacan suggested in Seminar III and, hence, it seems that, from a clinical perspective, the neurotic has the ability to tolerate uncertainty—uncertainty about one's sex, and the questions of procreation. While this tolerance comes with extravagant displays of dissatisfaction, complaint, demands, and a constant search for a master, the neurotic's search for answers is to be understood as her attempt at seeking to be complete. She is incomplete because she gave up that something that she never had to begin with. In other words, she gave up the position of being the maternal imaginary phallus with the hope of having it in the symbolic someday, although she never was the maternal phallus and neither will she receive that symbolic phallus she is hoping for. Something that she never had and never will have has been missing since her very entry into the symbolic. It is castration that marked this lack, which she repressed, and it is desire that keeps her going from object to object, seeking, obtaining, refusing, and seeking again. Even when certain objects might seem to be exactly what she is looking for, she will soon realise that nothing will serve as that missing piece. It is this structure of impossibility that perhaps gives a neurotic the strength to hold back their questions and tolerate the uncertainties. Without submitting to castration, it is impossible to tolerate one's existential questions and the disappointments of the human conditions, which is precisely what psychotics lack.

In the light of the discussions throughout this book, it is evident that the difference between the sexes is a question that all children begin asking in their infantile stage and, as adults, neurotics continue to ask. The questions I am about to ask are not psychoanalytic, although the subject hovers at the border between psychoanalysis and society. On the one hand, considering that there is a current upheaval in neutralising gender, so to speak (not a psychoanalytic term), which can be described as an urgency to remove differences between the sexes, it is evident that parental roles within a couple or a nuclear family are fast disappearing. Is there a connection between this phenomenon and the increased number of states of dissolution, depression, anxiety, and hopelessness? It seems as if tolerance of the uncertainties of the human condition is disappearing fast. On the other hand, with the increasing prevalence of ethical and political correctness, it seems that one's sexuality is not up for discussion as there is no room for doubt. The element of certainty involved in such discourses illustrates almost zero tolerance for any questioning of one's sex. How do we relate to such phenomena in the light of our current reading of Lacan's and Freud's theories on castration?

Food for thought

Considering Freud's work in *The Psychopathology of Everyday Life* (1901b), it can be argued that as long as we dream, take part in jokes, bungle actions, and commit slips of the tongue we are displaying psychopathologies. But then there are pathologies that require intervention, as they interfere with one's daily activities and cause a significant amount of suffering. Coming out of the Oedipus complex, the structure one can aim to reach that has the least pathologies involved is the structure of neurosis. It is the only structure where the name-of-the-father is accepted, as it is repressed in the unconscious. In perversion, the name-of-the-father is disavowed, and in the structure of psychosis it is foreclosed. Neurosis is the only structure where the mother is not perceived as *with phallus*. Lacan believes that there is no doubt that "whether male or female, it [the child] locates the phallus very early on and . . . generously grants it to the mother, whether or not in a mirror image, or in a double mirror image" (Lacan, 1993, p. 319). In the structure of perversion, the mother is still perceived with the phallus and in the structure of psychosis there seems to be only the mother and the child, but no phallus. Perversion is the only structure where the mother retains the phallus in the perception of the subject. Neurosis is the only structure where the questions of infantile sexual researches have been modified, sustained, and contained in sophisticated versions at the structural level of one's subjectivity. This is because, at some point at the beginning of the subject's entry into the symbolic, there was a guarantor who allowed the subject to assume that there is a father, and it is he who has the phallus, which is not up for negotiation. Although such a guarantor is the symbolic father, which could be the law of society, the norms of the clan, the rituals and myths of the culture or religion, Lacan still highlights the importance of the real father's intervention.

In the case of the structure of neurosis, it can be assumed that such an intervention of the real father did take place. Considering that the myths of current society are shifting rapidly, and the symbolic father is slowly becoming obsolete, who would be that guarantor? Lacan believes that the phallus is a "wanderer", it is always "elsewhere", but the father "is supposed to be the vehicle" of the phallus (Lacan, 1993, p. 319). The father must make it "impossible for the child to persist in trying to be the phallus for the mother" (Evans, 1996, p. 129). Is there not a similarity between Hans' father's willingness to accommodate and current society's urgency to broaden boundaries? Does the idea of a father (whether symbolic or real) in today's world seem to match with what Lacan is proposing? Lacan asserts that he not only has to castrate both the child and the mother, but also he must establish that he

> ... has his own and that's that, he neither exchanges it nor gives it. There is no circulation. The father has no function in the trio [mother–child–phallus], except to represent the vehicle, the holder, of the phallus. The father, as father, has the phallus—full stop. (Lacan, 1993, p. 319)

At the beginning of this chapter, I emphasised that it is Freud's drive theory along with all the disjunctions it represents with regard to the aim, direction, and object of the drive that indicates that human sexuality is inherently polymorphously perverse, such is the quality of infantile sexuality from which we begin as subjects. The demands of civilisation force us to give up such a perverse position, along with the real father's intervention, as Lacan's theories illustrate. In a broader sense, these demands are castration. If such demands are beginning to dissipate (both society and the real father), then there is very little hope of our libidinal reorganisation and giving up our infantile position. How does our society reflect in the light of this interpretation?

REFERENCES

American Psychiatric Association (2013). *Diagnostic and Statistical Manual of Mental Disorders* (5th edn) *(DSM-5)*. Washington, DC: American Psychiatric Publishing.

Brunswick, R. M. (1929). The analysis of a case of paranoia (delusion of jealousy). *Journal of Nervous and Mental Disease—An American Journal of Neuropsychiatry, 70*: 1–22.

Deutsch, H. (1944)[1932]. *The Psychology of Women*. New York: Grune & Stratton.

Evans, D. (1996). *An Introductory Dictionary of Lacanian Psychoanalysis*. New York: Routledge.

Fink, B. (1997). *A Clinical Introduction to Lacanian Psychoanalysis: Theory and Technique*. Cambridge and London: Harvard University Press.

Freud, S. (1900a). *The Interpretation of Dreams. S. E., 4–5*. London: Hogarth.

Freud, S. (1901b). *The Psychopathology of Everyday Life. S. E., 6*. London: Hogarth.

Freud, S. (1905d). *Three Essays on the Theory of Sexuality. S. E., 7*: 124–245. London: Hogarth.

Freud, S. (1905e). *Fragment of an Analysis of a Case of Hysteria. S. E., 7*: 3–122. London: Hogarth.

Freud, S. (1907c). The sexual enlightenment of children (An open letter to Dr. M. Furst). *S. E., 9*: 130–139. London: Hogarth.

Freud, S. (1908c). On the sexual theories of children. *S. E., 9*: 205–226. London: Hogarth.

Freud, S. (1909b). *Analysis of a Phobia in a Five-Year-Old-Boy. S. E., 10*: 3–149. London: Hogarth.

Freud, S. (1909d). *Notes upon a Case of Obsessional Neurosis. S. E., 10*: 153–249. London: Hogarth.

Freud, S. (1910h). A special type of choice of object made by men. *S. E., 11*: 163–176. London: Hogarth.

Freud, S. (1911c). *Psycho-analytic Notes on an Autobiographical Account of a Case of Paranoia. S. E., 12*: 3–82. London: Hogarth.

Freud, S. (1912–1913). *Totem and Taboo. S. E., 13*: 1–164. London: Hogarth.

Freud, S. (1913i). The disposition to obsessional neurosis. *S. E., 12*: 311–326. London: Hogarth.

Freud, S. (1914c). On narcissism: an introduction. *S. E., 14*: 67–107. London: Hogarth.

Freud, S. (1915c). Instincts and their vicissitudes. *S. E., 14*: 111–139. London: Hogarth.

Freud, S. (1916–1917). *Introductory Lectures on Psycho-Analysis Part III. S. E., 16*: 243–476. London: Hogarth.

Freud, S. (1918a). The taboo of virginity. *S. E., 11*: 191–208. London: Hogarth.

Freud, S. (1918b). *From the History of an Infantile Neurosis. S. E., 17*: 3–123. London: Hogarth.

Freud, S. (1919e). 'A child is being beaten'. A contribution towards the study of the origin of sexual perversion. *S. E., 17*: 177–204. London: Hogarth.

Freud, S. (1920a). The psychogenesis of a case of homosexuality in a woman. *S. E., 18*: 146–172. London: Hogarth.

Freud, S. (1920g). *Beyond the Pleasure Principle. S. E., 18*: 7–64. London: Hogarth.

Freud, S. (1921c). *Group Psychology and the Analysis of the Ego. S. E., 18*: 67–143. London: Hogarth.

Freud, S. (1923b). *The Ego and the Id. S. E., 19*: 3–68. London: Hogarth.

Freud, S. (1923e). The infantile genital organization. *S. E., 19*: 140–153. London: Hogarth.

Freud, S. (1924d). The dissolution of the Oedipus complex. *S. E., 19*: 172–179. London: Hogarth.

Freud, S. (1925h). Negation. *S. E., 19*: 234–239. London: Hogarth.

Freud, S. (1925j). Some psychical consequences of the anatomical distinction between the sexes. *S. E., 19*: 243–258. London: Hogarth.

Freud, S. (1926d). *Inhibitions, Symptoms and Anxiety. S. E.*, 20: 77–175. London: Hogarth.

Freud, S. (1926e). The question of lay analysis. *S. E.*, 20: 179–258. London: Hogarth.

Freud, S. (1930a). *Civilization and Its Discontents. S. E.*, 21: 59–145. London: Hogarth.

Freud, S. (1931b). Female sexuality. *S. E.*, 21: 223–243. London: Hogarth.

Freud, S. (1933a). *New Introductory Lectures on Psycho-Analysis. S. E.*, 22: 1–182. London: Hogarth.

Freud, S. (1937c). Analysis terminable and interminable. *S. E.*, 23: 216–254. London: Hogarth.

Freud, S. (1940a). *An Outline of Psycho-Analysis. S. E.*, 23: 141–207. London: Hogarth.

Freud, S. (1971)[1935]. Letter to Carl Muller-Braunschweig. Published as: Freud and female sexuality: a previously unpublished letter. *Psychiatry*, 34: 328–329.

Gallagher, C. (2006). From Freud's mythology of sexuality to Lacan's formulae of sexuation. *The Letter*, 38: 1–9.

Grigg, R. (1999). From the mechanism of psychosis to the universal condition of the symptom: on foreclosure. In: D. Nobus (Ed.), *Key Concepts of Lacanian Psychoanalysis* (pp. 48-74). New York: Other Press.

Jones, E. (1955). *Sigmund Freud: Life and Work Vol. 2 Years of Maturity 1901–1919*. London: Hogarth Press.

Lacan, J. (1957). *The Seminar of Jacques Lacan, Book IV: The Object Relation*, J.-A. Miller (Ed.), L. V. A. Roche (Trans.) (unpublished).

Lacan, J. (1958). *The Seminar of Jacques Lacan Book V: The Formations of the Unconscious*, C. Gallagher (Trans.). Available at: www.lacaninireland.ie.

Lacan, J. (1993). *The Seminar of Jacques Lacan Book III: The Psychoses*, R. Grigg (Ed.), J.-A. Miller (Trans.). New York: W. W. Norton.

Lacan, J. (2006a). On a question prior to any possible treatment of psychoanalysis. In: *Ecrits*, B. Fink (Trans.) (pp. 445–488). New York: W. W. Norton.

Lacan, J. (2006b). The signification of the phallus. In: B. Fink (Trans.), *Ecrits* (pp. 575–584). New York: W. W. Norton.

Lampl-de Groot, J. (1927). The evolution of the Oedipus complex in women. *International Journal of Psychoanalysis*, 9: 332–345.

Laplanche, J., & Pontalis, J.-B. (1973). *The Language of Psycho-Analysis*. New York: W. W. Norton.

Masson, J. M. (1984). *The Assault on Truth: Freud's Suppression of the Seduction Theory*. New York: Farrar, Straus and Giroux.

Nobus, D. (2000). *Jacques Lacan and the Freudian Practice of Psychoanalysis*. New York: Routledge.

Vanheule, S. (2014). *Diagnosis and the DSM: A Critical Review*. New York: Palgrave Macmillan.

Verhaeghe, P. (2000). The collapse of the function of the father and its effect on gender roles. In: R. Salecl (Ed.), *Sexuation* (pp. 131–154). Durham, NC: Duke University Press.

disposition, 88
group, 127–128
herd, 127
impulse, 68, 106
　feminine, 68, 70
　obscure, 60, 65
　passive, 106
interest, 88
life, 86, 88–92, 128
of mastery, 91
oral, 91
sadistic, 10
of scopophilia, 91
sexual, 10, 74, 90–91, 126, 128
theory of, 72–73, 75–76
transformation of, 88
wishes, 61
intervention, 13–15, 33, 39, 51,
　133–134, 137–140, 142, 144–145,
　153–154, 165, 170–172

jealousy, 24, 28, 31, 45, 49, 96–98, 100,
　127, 139
　delusional, 43, 111
　paranoia, 111
　violent, 111
Jones, E., xii, 6, 37, 43, 45, 154

Krafft-Ebing, R., 69

Lacan, J. (passim)
　cited works, xi, 6, 15, 131, 133 144,
　　147–156, 158, 160–168,
　　170–171
Lampl-de Groot, J., 40, 44,
　111–112
Laplanche, J., 2, 7–8, 70–71, 89,
　117–118, 128–129
libido, 23–24, 28, 31, 38, 43, 50, 60, 64,
　72, 76, 85, 89–90, 101, 112–114,
　118, 129, 148 see also: ego, object,
　oedipal
　child's, 53, 97
　female, 43, 112–113
　fixation of, 101–102, 135
　masculine, 64, 84, 113

masochism, 44, 86
　feminine, 44
　impulses, 84–86
　wishes, 114
Masson, J. M., 12
masturbation, 26, 28–29, 52, 89, 105,
　143
　activity, 53, 105
　clitoral, 28, 30, 50, 57, 61, 76, 103,
　　105–106
　compulsion to, 29
　confession of, 28
　early, 105
　habits, 61
　infantile, 25–26, 50–51, 105
　jouissance, 152
　masculine, 29
　prohibition of, 51–53, 57

narcissism, 27, 117–118, 123, 134, 163
　bond, 124
　cathexis, 33
　ideal, 120
　investment, 25, 47
　object-choice, 117–119, 124, 127
　original, 118
Nobus, D., 161

object(ive) (passim) see also:
　narcissism
　of affection, 24
　bad, 155
　of castration, 22
　-cathexis, 92, 98
　change of, 44, 61, 104, 106, 127
　choice, xi, 11, 24, 28, 40, 44, 49, 52,
　　60, 108, 110, 114, 117–121, 134,
　　157
　anaclitic, 118
　future, 157
　homosexual, 47
　primitive, 30
　father-, 60–61, 95, 108–109
　fetish, 154
　first, 24
　good, 155

For Product Safety Concerns and Information please contact our EU
representative GPSR@taylorandfrancis.com
Taylor & Francis Verlag GmbH, Kaufingerstraße 24, 80331 München, Germany

* 9 7 8 1 7 8 2 2 0 5 8 0 7 *